Lipsmackin' Backpackin'

Lightweight, Trail-tested Recipes for Backcountry Trips

Tim and Christine Conners

ThreeForks

Guilford, Connecticut
An imprint of The Globe Pequot Press

We dedicate this book to the dozens of outdoor adventurers who generously gave of their time and energy to submit their favorite recipes and ideas and assist us in our efforts. Our book would not have been possible without your help and encouragement. May you especially be blessed by the benediction found in Psalm 18:33:

May the Lord God make your feet like those of a deer and enable you to stand upon the high places.

Library of Congress Cataloging-in-Publication Data
Connors, Christine.
   Lipsmackin' backpackin' : lightweight, trail-tested recipes for backcountry
trips / Christine and Tim Connors
      p. cm. —
   ISBN 1-56044-881-4 (pbk.)
   1. Outdoor cookery. I. Conners, Tim. II. Title.
TX823 .C633 2000
641.5'78—dc21   99-054507

Manufactured in Canada
First Edition / Fourth Printing

Contents

Acknowledgments

Editors of outdoor newsletters from around the country graciously printed our requests for recipe submissions. Webmasters for several large trail organizations built links to our automatic recipe submission page. Our requests for ideas were posted through major outdoor Internet bulletin boards. We dropped recipe submission forms at trail resupply points up and down the Sierra Nevada and in trail register boxes at road crossings and post offices. We would jokingly threaten our long-distance backpacking guests with abandonment far from the trailhead unless they gave us their best ideas. Each source was a very important avenue through which we received much valuable input. For the hundreds, if not thousands, of folks who endured our relentless badgering, we are grateful for your good humor and patience. For those who assisted the cause by contributing recipes and ideas or by helping others to do so, we can never thank you enough. There would be no book without you.

Of course, certain people were particularly helpful in our efforts. Bob Ballou, executive director of the Pacific Crest Trail Association, and Lee Terkelsen, editor of the Pacific Crest Trail Association's *The Communicator*, worked overtime to help spread the word of our need for recipe submissions. This very deserving volunteer trail association was a continuous source of assistance and encouragement to us during the entire duration of the project. Butch and Peggy Wiggs, proprietors of the Vermilion Valley Resort, beat the drums for our book throughout the High Sierra. Kathleen Cutshall was helpful in kitchen testing several of the recipes, and Chet Fromm was instrumental in assisting us with our website and bringing to our attention the value of the Internet for gathering additional ideas for the book. To all of you, endless thanks.

Introduction

I collapsed in a stupor against the side of a fallen pine high in the Sierra Nevada Mountains of California on the banks of Deer Creek. After weeks of grinding northward along the John Muir Trail, my bones and tendons screamed in unified agony. I was utterly spent. My will to continue would have been nonexistent had it not been for visions of the culinary wonders that awaited only a few hours ahead in the town of Mammoth Lakes, my next resupply point. It had been two weeks since I last ate food other than the revolting fare found in my backpack, and I craved something, *anything,* from a restaurant. I had brought along thirty pounds of rations that now occupied a very different place in my heart than when I first started the trip. As the days passed, I was eating less and less of the nutrient-laden fare that my body desperately needed simply because I couldn't tolerate the taste any longer. At a time when my body's metabolism was moving into overdrive and requiring even more and better fuel, I was in a downward nutritional spiral that was affecting not only my physical health but beginning to affect my mental health as well.

As I leaned against the downed pine, I caught a glimpse over my left shoulder of the gleaming side of a Pepsi truck parked behind the trees in a shady flat. I was elated, thinking that a country store must be nearby. No more daydreaming! I was about to feast on ice cream and soda after all those days of depravation. I turned around to gather my equipment. Through my mental fog, it occurred to me that it was unlikely to find a cola truck so deep in the mountain wilderness. No! I turned back around to ensure that what I had seen was real. The beautiful truck was still there! But as I prepared to lift my aching body from its resting place, my newfound oasis faded from sight. With many miles yet to go, I sat there in self-pity, having been completely hoodwinked by what was the most vivid hallucination I had ever experienced. In hindsight, I shouldn't have been so surprised: Two days earlier, under a hot noon sun, I had heard the enchanting, endless melody of an ice cream truck while stumbling along the trail above Bear Creek. At the time, I was ten thousand feet above sea level and a dozen miles from the nearest road.

The power of food over our physical health and well-being is evident to most people, if not taken for granted. Its strong psychological influences are not as well appreciated, but they're just as real. During my John Muir Trail trip, I was new to backpacking, and my in-the-field lesson dramatically demonstrated that food issues can easily make or break a long-duration backcountry outing. I was fortunate in that I experienced my nutritionally induced crash close to a town with a wide selection of provisions. Once in Mammoth Lakes, I was able to take advantage of a vast array of new supplies in order to completely revamp and enliven my backpacking menu. Had the problems occurred earlier, I likely would have had to leave the mountains altogether and end the trip prematurely. Instead, having stocked myself with a new and satisfying food repertoire, I was able to continue on to Yosemite Valley and complete the Muir Trail.

For short-duration trips, spanning one or two nights on the trail, most folks, even those with little experience, can throw together an adequate menu that will meet their needs. However, for those who are planning longer trips lasting from several days to several months, few are immune to the havoc wreaked by a poorly planned or improperly stocked backpacking menu. The total weight of the food becomes far more important as does the taste, nutritional value, variety, and simplicity of the menu, so the planning aspects grow correspondingly more difficult as one attempts to balance these five key parameters. While preparing for the Muir Trail, I was able to keep the total weight of my food to a manageable amount. However, I made two important assumptions with respect to my backpacking menu that reflected a lack of experience: First, in keeping the menu simple, I felt it necessary to have little variety; second, in order to keep the meals nutritious, I believed I would have to trade taste. Both were critical mistakes that nearly cost me my goal.

During the years when we lived near the Pacific Crest National Scenic Trail in the Tehachapi Mountains of California, Christine and I would often host long-distance hikers coming through the area on their way north or south. "What do you eat while on the trail?" was one of the questions that we would always ask our guests out of curiosity. We both had hundreds of miles of hiking experience by that time, but we could not fathom the concept of happily eating from one's backpack for *months* on end. These folks apparently knew something that we didn't. We discovered that their secret was consistent and should have been obvious: They knew *exactly* what they liked to eat while on the trail, and, of course, their recipes formed the cornerstone for the secret.

As I learned on the Muir Trail, discovering what recipes and food preparation ideas work best is not necessarily an easy lesson. We wanted to learn from those with the most experience, so Christine and I began collecting recipes and tips from our long-distance backpacking acquaintances. We figured their food ideas had to work well, having powered these folks through very difficult conditions spanning thousands of miles. It didn't take long to realize that this small treasure chest of recipes and tips was worth turning into a book. We felt that a collection of ideas from people with such significant experience would not only benefit the trail community in general but, in particular, those who wished to spend more than a couple of nights in the backcountry. What began as a small collection of long-distance, long-duration hiking recipes became the foundation for this book. These pages now represent several years of effort collecting favorite recipes and food preparation ideas from experienced backcountry adventurers from around the world.

In this book, you will find a wide selection of recipes ranging from the simple to the gourmet, all requiring only common gear for final preparation in the wilderness. Of particular interest to the very long-distance backpacker, many can be prepared at home far in advance and stored for months prior to use. Complete instructions are included for each recipe, but unlike most backcountry cookbooks, key nutritional data and the pack-ready weight for each is also included. Having all of this information together in one source will help you identify your own unique balance between the five key trail-food parameters: weight, taste, nutritional value, variety, and simplicity.

This book presents a broad range of recipes and food preparation ideas from which you, whether experienced or aspiring, can construct a unique and satisfying trail menu. Perhaps you will use the book's ideas simply as a springboard from which to build a completely customized repertoire. Regardless of how you use this book, it is with sincere hope that these trail-tested recipes and tips will reduce the otherwise typical anxieties, uncertainties, and hassles of planning your menu and packing your food while lengthening your list of favorite trail recipes. May it help you increase your days and miles in the backcountry and, in doing so, make your time on the trail, no matter how long, more enjoyable.

Tim Conners
Cincinnati, Ohio

About the Book

The recipes in this book are grouped according to the meals during which they most likely will be eaten. If you do not see what you are looking for in one meal group, try searching another. All recipes contain complete ingredient lists and the steps for preparation. Many recipes require pretrip preparation at home, with final preparation in the backcountry. Complete instructions, for home and backcountry, are included.

So you won't have to carry this book with you and to simplify final recipe preparation in the backcountry, "Packable Trailside Cooking Instructions" are included in the back of this book. This section is intended to be torn out and taken along on the trip. You can either tear out the entire section and create your own lightweight, packable book of trailside cooking instructions or cut out individual instructions and place the slips of paper in your bag of ingredients or another convenient place in your pack. The Packable Trailside Cooking Instructions are also available online at www.Falconbooks.com/lipsmackin. Reference the Packable Trailside Cooking Instructions by recipe name.

Oftentimes, the contributor provided an interesting story related to his or her experience with the recipe he or she gave us. If so, we've included the story along with the recipe. In doing so, we believe that you will find the information interesting and will more fully appreciate the recipe in light of the circumstances in which it has been used in the past. The contributor's name and hometown can be found at the bottom of each recipe.

Four examples of meal systems are included. Meal systems provide for a flexible use of a fixed amount of basic staples and can simplify pretrip menu planning while providing variety on the trail. Novel food preparation ideas and valuable tips can be found in individual recipes throughout the book. Look for authors' notes for additional information about individual recipes as well.

If your curiosity with respect to long-distance trekking has been piqued, or if you are an accomplished long-distance adventurer looking for new challenges, we've included information on the National Scenic and Historic Trails managed by the Departments of Agriculture and Interior, along with addresses and phone numbers through which you will be able to obtain additional information. Associations, web pages, and e-mail newsgroups specific to the trail of interest are often valuable sources of information as well. A map of the United States showing the location of each trail is also provided.

Using the Recipes

Servings

We have estimated how many average-size servings each recipe will produce. Of course, the definition of "average" is subjective, and our use of serving units is intended to serve only as a consistent reference between recipes. You should carefully consider your own individual appetite and nutritional needs. If you will be on the trail for many days or weeks, your appetite may grow significantly with time. What would be a satisfying meal for you at the beginning of the trip might only be the first course days later.

Weight Values

For each recipe, a weight value is given for individual servings as well as for the recipe as a whole. You should translate these values as necessary to any customized serving size to be used in the backcountry. The weight values represent the pack-ready ingredients. They do not include the weight of any filtered water that may be required for preparation.

Nutritional Information

The nutritional information included in this book is intended to serve as a starting point for evaluating the overall dietary value of a particular menu. Calorie, carbohydrate, protein, fiber, fat, sodium, and cholesterol data are included for each recipe in order to help you balance each according to your own nutritional requirements. We suggest that you become familiar with your own backcountry needs so that you do not leave critical nutrients out of your menu while on your trips.

Keep in mind that even though you may have a perfect balance between carbohydrates, proteins, and fats, along with the correct number of calories and the proper amount of fiber, your body also requires a large amount of vitamins, minerals, and micronutrients. Although supplements can help meet the body's daily requirements for these nutrients, a menu rich in vegetables and fruits, dehydrated or fresh, is also advisable. The demands of long-distance trekking are so great on the body that top-quality food must be the rule and not the exception.

Note that the nutritional information presented in this book could change depending on your choice of product brands or ingredient substitution.

Temperature

All temperatures are presented in degrees Fahrenheit.

Recommendations and Tips

Equipment

Food Scale

We have attempted to save you effort by providing the weights and measures for each recipe. However, if your customized serving sizes consistently differ from those in this book, having a food scale handy can help you quickly and accurately apportion each recipe for the appropriate serving size while providing information for the total combined weight of the food to be carried in the pack. Knowing the exact weight will also help you convert the nutritional data for a standard serving to that of a customized serving.

Food Processor

A food processor, though not required, is useful for reducing the amount of effort spent preparing and slicing food. A processor will also keep the slice sizes consistent. This is particularly useful if a large quantity of food is to be processed or if the food is to be dried in a dehydrator.

Blender

A blender is useful for puréeing foods prior to drying. For example, a blender can easily reduce a chunky spaghetti sauce to a smooth consistency in order to produce a thin roll of sauce leather. This will speed up both the dehydration and the rehydration processes.

Stove and Trail Cookware

The range of cookware and stoves available for trail use is enormous, and very few people have the same preference when it comes to pots, fry pans, cooking and eating utensils, and stoves. A description of all the types on the market is beyond the scope of this book, and even a recommendation as to which to carry on the trail is fraught with peril because of individual preferences and will not be undertaken here.

We do recommend, however, that you carefully consider your own eating and cooking preferences before buying any type of cooking equipment. For the person who likes to use a fry pan primarily, it would be unwise to use a stove with a narrow base, as it will tip easily under the wide diameter of the pan and the aggressive utensil action required for frying. Some stoves have a very narrow throttle range, so if you desire to cook delicacies in the wilderness, you would want to avoid those stoves that operate only as a blast furnace. A stackable set of small pots makes sense for the chef who prefers to make a variety of different foods at each meal, whereas a single larger pot works for the person who is content with a single dish at any one time. Think through your preferred eating habits and choose your equipment accordingly.

Look for equipment that can be used for more than one purpose so that you can bring the least amount of equipment possible. This will lighten your load, reduce your pack volume, and simplify your cleanup after the meal. For example, wide-mouth plastic bottles can function as drinking jars, food rehydrating containers, and measuring cups. Experiment, practice, and be open to new and better ideas.

Pack Oven

A few of the recipes in this book recommend the use of a backpack oven for final preparation. The ultralight versions are relatively inexpensive and weigh only a few ounces. If dough mixes do not comprise a significant portion of your trail food, a pack oven may not be necessary. However, if you are looking for a change in your trail food repertoire or are a great fan of baked goods, you will probably find that an oven is a welcome addition to your pack. Procedures for preparing dough mixes will vary depending on your choice of oven, but specific instructions will be included with the unit you select.

Food Dehydrator

If you plan on preparing a large variety of backcountry foods, a dehydrator is a great investment. Dehydrating foods is a relatively simple way to enhance the flavor, nutritional value, and variety of your trail meals while also reducing your pack weight. A dehydrator removes much of the water from a food product, which can greatly extend its unrefrigerated shelf life. Dehydrating can reduce fresh food weight by as much as 90 percent and is a less costly, more flavorful alternative to buying preprocessed, commercially available, freeze-dried meals-in-a-pouch. A dehydrator opens the door to a large realm of delicious foods that can be hard to find in outdoor supply stores and catalogs. Many of the recipes in this book call for the use of dehydrated food, and frankly, the backcountry adventurer's menu will be greatly limited without the availability of such.

Although some drying can be performed in a kitchen oven, we recommend you consider one of the many commercially available dehydrators. A dehydrator containing a fan blower along with a thermostat will typically provide more consistency and higher quality in the dried product than units without them because the fan helps eliminate hot spots. Accessories such as special trays that simplify the drying of liquids and other unique food items can be very useful.

Practice drying a variety of foods in order to learn the nuances of your machine. Most commercially available units will come with an instruction manual showing you how to best dehydrate different types of food. Keep in mind that the thinner the food is sliced, the more quickly and thoroughly it will dry and the sooner it will rehydrate. Food that is underdried will contain more moisture and therefore will spoil more quickly than if it had been dried thoroughly. For an enjoyable trip, and for your own health and safety, it is important that you dry your food properly. Practice using your dehydrator and become proficient with it before you first use it for a backcountry trip.

Need additional persuasion that dehydrating foods is worth the effort? What follows is just some of the enthusiastic input that we received on the subject from our contributors.

> I used a dehydrator to dry vegetables and spaghetti sauce. Spread frozen mixed vegetables on trays before going to bed at night; in the morning, you'll have days' worth of vegetables. Our food rehydrated wonderfully in the backpack. Just add water to the food in a well-sealing plastic container with a lid about an hour or so before dinner.
>
> DIANE ARNOLD
> SOMERS, CONNECTICUT

> When I bought a food dryer in the early 1980s, a whole new realm of backpacking meals became available to me. I discovered that I could precook rice or pasta and dry it. Then it required no further cooking on the trail. It merely needed to be generously covered with filtered water; in an hour or two, it would be fully rehydrated. Whoopee! Rice and pasta salads galore!
>
> PAM COZ-HILL
> VISALIA, CALIFORNIA

> What really gave our meals some pizzazz were the dehydrated veggies, i.e. green beans, mushrooms, red onions, carrots, and corn. This, along with a three-foot-long pepperoni, made our meals gourmet.
>
> DAN AND TINA BREEDLOVE
> "THE HONEYMOONERS"
> EUDORA, KANSAS

Dehydrated strawberries made our oatmeal terrific.

DAN AND SARA RUFNER
SAN DIEGO, CALIFORNIA

A food dehydrator is very helpful for making meals. Frozen vegetables dry quickly and last a long time. Canned white meat chicken is great to dry. When I arrive in camp, I always place dried meat and vegetables in a small amount of water and allow it to soak while I enjoy the afternoon. By mealtime, it is tender and ready to add to the meal.

URSULA BROWER
SOUTH LAKE TAHOE, CALIFORNIA

Drying Tips

• To reduce the risk of bacterial contamination of the food, always clean and rinse your hands, work area, dehydrator, and utensils thoroughly before drying.

• The typical drying temperature ranges between 125° and 145° and varies according to the food being dried.

• When packaging your dried food, identify each item as it is bagged along with the date that it was dried. Make sure to first eat the food that has been stored for the longest time. When packing for your trip and cooking in the field, ensure that your dehydrated food hasn't spoiled. This is especially critical if you use food containing dairy products, eggs, or meats.

• Package your dried food very tightly to ensure that no moisture can enter the container. If moisture does enter, the food will begin to rehydrate and will then spoil much faster. *Never use food that is even beginning to look or smell rancid.*

• Store <u>cooled</u> dried food in moistureproof containers or sealed bags and place them in a cool, dry, and dark place. Food dried at home can normally be stored at room temperature for up to two months, in a refrigerator for up to six months, and in a freezer for up to one year. Heavy-duty resealable plastic bags work well for both storage and trail use.

• It is better to store and carry dehydrated foods in individual, meal-size bags and containers. Avoid storing multimeal amounts of food in a single container or bag, as the repeated openings and closings could compromise the seal, allowing the remaining food to spoil more quickly.

• Ensure that products containing dried eggs, dairy, and meats are thoroughly cooked prior to drying. Salting the final product will help preserve the food.

Keep these types of food frozen until you are ready for your trip.

- Place pieces of cut food on drying trays in such a way that air will circulate all around the food. Do not permit items to overlap; otherwise, the drying will be inconsistent among the pieces.

- Check food on an hourly basis when you are first learning the nuances of your dehydrator. Some dehydrators may require rotating the food pieces or trays in order to speed up the drying process or to prevent inconsistent drying.

- Avoid mixing foods with different aromas when drying them; otherwise, flavors may transfer. For example, if spaghetti sauce were to be dried with peaches, the flavor of the sauce would be transferred to the peaches.

- When drying aromatic foods, your house will be completely filled with the aroma. This is something to consider if you don't enjoy the smell of a particular food, such as onions.

- Cook pasta, beans, and rice at home and dehydrate them before your trip. They will rehydrate quickly on the trail and require far less time and fuel to heat. If you don't want to carry a stove, you can rehydrate these without heat to make a cold pasta, bean, or rice salad.

- You can dry thick liquids or pastes on a sheet of plastic wrap or wax paper placed over a dehydrator tray. Freshly poured pools of liquids or pastes should be kept under ¼ inch in depth.

- If a tray's mesh size is too large, smaller pieces of food, such as rice, can be dried on a piece of cheesecloth or plastic wrap placed over the tray.

- Meats should be thoroughly cooked, cut into very small pieces or shredded, and rinsed under hot water to remove as much fat as possible prior to drying. In addition, use higher drying temperatures of 140º to 145º. In doing both, you help ensure that the meat is dried completely and safely prior to packaging.

- Frozen, canned, or fresh vegetables can all be dried with success. If drying fresh vegetables, ensure that they are ripe, clean, and free of bruises. Prior to drying, blanching is required for most fresh vegetables in order to stop an enzymatic action that can cause spoilage. This can be accomplished by steaming the vegetables until slightly tender but not fully cooked. Stir the vegetables frequently during the blanching process. Onions, mushrooms, and tomatoes do not require blanching. Dry vegetables at 130º. Vegetables will normally feel somewhat brittle when dried.

- Cooking certain families of vegetables, such as legumes, corn, and roots (such as carrots), prior to drying will reduce the time required for rehydration and cooking on the trail.

- Like vegetables, fruit can also be dried whether first obtained frozen, canned, or fresh. Ensure that fresh fruit is ripe, clean, and free of bruises and pits. To minimize browning during the drying process, allow fruit to first soak for 5 minutes in a mixture of ¼ cup lemon juice to 1 quart of water. Dry fruits at 135º. Dried fruits will normally have a leathery texture and be somewhat chewy.

Rehydrating

Rehydrating is simply the process of putting the water back into food and returning it to its normal consistency. The rehydration process varies depending on the type of food. In some instances, simply adding some water to a dehydrated meal may be enough to rehydrate it. In other instances, you may need to heat the water and the dehydrated food together to ensure full rehydration. The length of time it takes dehydrated food to rehydrate will also depend on the type of food, how finely chopped it is, and the cooking altitude. Because these factors can vary greatly, we have included general directions for how to rehydrate each applicable recipe in this book.

Planning and Preparation Tips

• Premix ingredients to the maximum extent possible before you leave on your trip. This will simplify your food preparation in the field.

• Carry a plastic container that doubles as a measuring cup. If graduations are not included on the container, make your own prior to the trip by etching the container for appropriate measurements such as a quarter, half, and full cup.

• Learn to approximate one teaspoon and one tablespoon in your pack spoon.

• When packaging a meal, label the container with a description of the contents along with information necessary to complete the preparation in the field, such as the amount of water required to rehydrate or the amount of oil necessary to fry.

• If using boxed, store-bought food on the trail, transfer the contents of the box to a smaller container if possible. Be sure to cut out the directions from the box and package them with the food for use on the trail. Trailside instructions are also available at www.Falconbooks.com/lipsmackin.

• Carry a selection of spices with you on every trip. Experiment with them and tailor your collection to fit your own taste. Besides salt and pepper, some of the more common spices include cinnamon, oregano, curry, garlic, cumin, basil, cayenne, and thyme.

• Collect condiment packages for your trips. They provide an easy way to liven up a meal. Ketchup, mustard, mayonnaise, and relish are often readily available, but soy sauce, Parmesan cheese, dried red peppers, salsa, and barbecue sauce can also be found. Be careful that the condiments don't spoil. Some, such as mayonnaise, have a relatively short shelf life.

Breakfast

Pacific Crest Pancakes

4 cups of flour

¾ cup powdered buttermilk

½ cup Backpacker's Pantry
   Scrambled Egg Mix

1 tablespoon baking soda

1 tablespoon Crisco per
   serving

½ cup water per serving

Total weight: 2 pounds 12 ounces
Weight per serving: 4 ounces
Total servings: 11 (2 pancakes per serving)

At home:
Stir all dry ingredients together well, mashing out lumps. Divide mix into 11 individual servings of ½ cup each. Store in individual resealable plastic bags. Carry Crisco separately.

On the trail:
Melt Crisco in pan. Add ½ cup water to one bag (½ cup) of mix. Knead in bag. To cook, spoon or pour pancake batter into the greased cooking pan. Turn once. Since pancakes can burn easily on backpacking stoves, adjust the flame to its lowest setting and be prepared to hold the pan above the flame if it gets too hot.

Our plan for the Pacific Crest Trail was to have an occasional pancake breakfast for variety. But making pancakes, and cleaning up, takes a lot of time. We weren't willing to spend that time in the mornings; we wanted to get out of camp and on the trail. So we ended up making these pancakes in the evening as "bread" to go along with dinner.

When planning this hike, my hiking partner Lee had dreamed of fried-fish dinners, so we were carrying a small quantity of Crisco. There's not much time to fish either when you're trying to make 18 to 20 miles each day, so we had surplus Crisco. We fried the pancakes in ever-increasing amounts of frying oil as our bodies depleted their fat reserves. We were often so hungry that we didn't give the pancakes enough time to cook through. We didn't care just so that they held together long enough for us to eat them! Lee always took the last pancake and sopped up all the melted Crisco in the pan.

ANN MARSHALL
PORT ORCHARD, WASHINGTON

Nutritional information per serving

calories	290
protein	6 g
carbohydrates	33 g
sodium	380 mg
fiber	0 g
fat	15 g
cholesterol	33 mg

Whole-Wheat Palisades Pancakes with Syrup

Total weight: 1 pound 4 ounces
Weight per serving: 4 ounces
Total servings: 5

At home:

In a large bowl, mix together all dry pancake mix ingredients. Place ½ cup of the mixture into each of five resealable plastic bags.

For the syrup mix, place 2 tablespoons brown sugar into each of five resealable plastic bags. Place one sealed bag of brown sugar into each of the five bags of pancake mix.

Store butter and water separately.

On the trail:

To make a single serving, melt 1 tablespoon butter in pan. Remove brown sugar bag from bag of pancake mix. Add approximately ½ cup water to pancake mix. Knead bag until no lumps remain in batter. Cut a large hole in one corner of the bag and pour into pan. Watch pancake carefully and flip when the first side has browned.

Add 1 tablespoon water to brown sugar in bag and knead mixture until all lumps disappear. Pour the syrup onto a cooked pancake.

TIM AND CHRISTINE CONNERS
CINCINNATI, OHIO

Pancake mix:

2 tablespoons powdered eggs

1½ cups powdered buttermilk

½ teaspoon salt

½ cup cornmeal

1 cup whole-wheat flour

½ teaspoon baking soda

2 teaspoons baking powder

A little less than ½ cup of water per serving

Syrup:

2 tablespoons brown sugar per serving

1 tablespoon water per serving

1 tablespoon butter per serving

Nutritional information per serving

calories	450
protein	18 g
carbohydrates	70 g
sodium	760 mg
fiber	3 g
fat	14 g
cholesterol	54 mg

Blue Ridge Blueberry Pancakes

1 cup whole-wheat flour

½ cup stone-ground yellow cornmeal

3 tablespoons powdered buttermilk

2 tablespoons powdered egg whites

1½ tablespoons granulated sugar

1½ teaspoons baking powder

¾ teaspoon baking soda

½ teaspoon ground cinnamon

½ teaspoon salt

½ cup dried blueberries

⅓ cup finely chopped almonds

¼ cup water per serving

¼ teaspoon canola oil per serving to add to mix

1 teaspoon canola oil per serving for greasing skillet

Pancake syrup (optional)

Total weight: 1 pound
Weight per serving: 4 ounces
Total servings: 4 (2 pancakes per serving)

At home:

In a large bowl, combine flour, cornmeal, powdered buttermilk, powdered egg whites, sugar, baking powder, baking soda, cinnamon, salt, blueberries, and almonds. Divide equally into four resealable plastic bags. Pour oil and syrup (if using) into separate small plastic containers.

On the trail:

For each serving, pour ¼ cup water and ¼ teaspoon canola oil directly into one bag of pancake mix and knead mixture well. Let stand 15 minutes. Grease skillet with 1 teaspoon canola oil, then place over medium heat. Cook pancakes until one side is light brown, then flip and cook until other side is browned. Serve with syrup, if desired.

CATHY CZACHOROWSKI
TORRINGTON, CONNECTICUT

Nutritional information per serving

calories	320
protein	11 g
carbohydrates	49 g
sodium	610 mg
fiber	8 g
fat	11 g
cholesterol	4 mg

Cameron Canyon Caramel Rolls

Total weight: 12 ounces
Weight per serving: 6 ounces
Total servings: 2

1 (8-ounce) package Jiffy
    Buttermilk Biscuit Mix
$\frac{1}{4}$ cup chopped pecans
$\frac{1}{4}$ cup brown sugar
2 tablespoons butter
$\frac{1}{2}$ cup water

At home:
Place biscuit mix in a sandwich bag. Mix pecans together with brown sugar and store in a separate, similar-size bag. Store butter separately.

On the trail:
Add the water to bag of biscuit mix and knead dough in bag. On low heat, melt butter in a frying pan, preferably one having a nonstick surface. Add sugar and pecans to butter and stir. Cut a hole at the bottom of the biscuit bag and squeeze out dough as thinly as possible on top of pecan, brown sugar, and butter mixture. Cover entire pan and allow to cook. Check frequently to ensure that sugar mixture is not burning. Dough will eventually become more biscuitlike. After allowing to cool, eat directly out of the pan.

We borrowed this recipe from the Hughes Family, friends of ours from Tehachapi, California.

TIM AND CHRISTINE CONNERS
CINCINNATI, OHIO

Nutritional information per serving

calories	780
protein	10 g
carbohydrates	117 g
sodium	1,240 mg
fiber	2 g
fat	33 g
cholesterol	37 mg

Backcountry Cinnamon Rolls

½ cup powdered sugar

2 tablespoons cinnamon

3 tablespoons chopped pecans

1½ cups Bisquick

⅛ cup powdered buttermilk

3 tablespoons margarine

⅓ cup water

Total weight: 13 ounces
Weight per serving: 6.5 ounces
Total servings: 2

At home:
Mix together sugar, cinnamon, and nuts and store in a resealable plastic bag. In a 1-gallon resealable plastic bag, mix Bisquick and powdered buttermilk. Store margarine separately. (Margarine in a squeeze bottle packs well.) Remember to bring a pack oven!

On the trail:
Add margarine to the sugar-cinnamon-nut mix and mush together. Add water to Bisquick-buttermilk mix and knead in bag. Take the dough out of the bag, place it on a flat surface, and work it into a square about 10 to 12 inches wide and ¼- to ⅛-inch thick (thinner is better). A sturdy water bottle can be used as a rolling pin. Spread the sugary paste evenly over the dough. Roll the dough into a log. Cut the log into 1-inch-wide portions and place slices side by side in your backpacking oven. Follow directions specific to your particular oven and allow to cook until the buns rise and become firm. Remove from the stove and let cool.

I owe this recipe to a backpacking buddy of mine named Scott Norton.

JEFFREY HARE
CITRUS HEIGHTS, CALIFORNIA

Nutritional information per serving

calories	650
protein	10 g
carbohydrates	92 g
sodium	1,180 mg
fiber	4 g
fat	28 g
cholesterol	5 mg

Big River Apricot Granola

Total weight: 2 pounds 5 ounces
Weight per serving: 5.3 ounces
Total servings: 7

At home:

Heat oil, honey, and syrup until thin. Add vanilla, yeast, wheat germ, oats, wheat, and rye, stirring well after each addition. Spread on cookie sheet and bake at 250° for 1½ to 2 hours. Stir periodically. Cool, then mix in fruits, nuts, and seeds. Store in airtight containers in a cool, dry place until used.

On the trail:

Eat as is or with powdered milk and water, either hot or cold. Serving size is about 1 cup per person. This is a very hearty and nutritional breakfast.

BRIAN GULDBERG
BOZEMAN, MONTANA

- ¼ cup canola oil
- ¼ cup honey
- ¼ cup maple syrup (can be substituted with sorghum or molasses)
- 1½ teaspoons vanilla
- 1 tablespoon nutritional yeast
- ½ cup wheat germ
- 2½ cups rolled oats
- 1 cup rolled wheat
- 1 cup rolled rye
- ½ cup unsweetened shredded coconut
- 1 cup Ocean Spray Craisins
- 1 cup chopped dried apricots
- ½ cup chopped dates
- ⅓ cup chopped almonds
- ½ cup unsalted sunflower seeds
- Powdered milk and water (optional)

I have found that grits provide good energy, cook up just fine, and taste good. By the last months of my Pacific Crest Trail thru-hike, I had given up on dehydrated hash browns and wheat noodles because they didn't seem to have the energy content that the rice and grits had.

CHARLIE THORPE
HUNTSVILLE, ALABAMA

Nutritional information per serving

calories	680
protein	16 g
carbohydrates	107 g
sodium	30 mg
fiber	12 g
fat	19 g
cholesterol	0 mg

Goose's Multigrain Granola

8 tablespoons (1 stick)
    melted margarine

½ cup brown sugar

1 teaspoon salt

1 teaspoon vanilla

½ cup water

2 cups rolled oats

2 cups rolled barley

2 cups rolled rye

2 cups rolled wheat

(Oats, barley, rye, and
    wheat may be
    substituted with 8
    cups uncooked
    Quaker Multigrain)

1 cup wheat germ

1 cup shredded
    sweetened coconut

¼ cup sesame seeds

½ cup chopped walnuts

Total weight: 2 pounds 8 ounces
Weight per serving: 4 ounces
Total servings: 10

At home:

Combine melted margarine, brown sugar, salt, vanilla, and water and stir over low heat until dissolved. Add oats, barley, rye, wheat, wheat germ, coconut, sesame seeds, and walnuts. Stir until moistened. Spread on two ungreased cookie sheets and bake for 2 hours at 250º to 275º. Stir occasionally with fork. May be packaged together or stored as ten separate 1-cup servings.

On the trail:

Add your own milk to 1 cup of granola mix in bowl or eat dry, straight from the bag.

This can be eaten dry, with milk, or as a hot breakfast by pouring boiling water over it. When I ate it hot, I added squeeze-margarine and brown sugar.

KATHLEEN CUTSHALL
"THE OLD GRAY GOOSE"
CONNEAUT, OHIO

Nutritional information per serving

calories	510
protein	15 g
carbohydrates	73 g
sodium	360 mg
fiber	12 g
fat	21 g
cholesterol	0 mg

Backpacking Cereal

Total weight: 1 pound 9 ounces
Weight per serving: 5 ounces
Total servings: 5

At home:

Mix all dry ingredients together in a bowl, then add oil and blend well. Store in an airtight container. It doesn't have to be refrigerated. Ready to eat as is, or it can be roasted like granola at 275° for 1 to 2 hours, stirring occasionally.

On the trail:

Eat 1 cup of cereal with water and powdered milk.

This mix is what my hiking partner Lee has eaten nearly every morning for breakfast, on the trail or at home, for the last 25 years. On the trail, while my stomach was grumbling and empty by midmorning, he had fuel enough to keep him going until lunch. This cereal is very filling, so start with a small amount each day until your system adjusts to it.

ANN MARSHALL
PORT ORCHARD, WASHINGTON

Regular dry oatmeal turned in a blender can be used as instant oatmeal on the trail.

IRWIN REEVES
BEAUMONT, CALIFORNIA

2 cups quick oats

1 cup wheat germ

1 cup whole-wheat flour

$\frac{1}{4}$ cup loose-packed brown sugar (or to taste)

1 cup finely chopped walnuts

$\frac{3}{4}$ cup vegetable oil

Water and powdered milk

Nutritional information per serving

calories	760
carbohydrates	64 g
protein	17 g
sodium	1 mg
fiber	10 g
fat	52 g
cholesterol	0 mg

Kooger's Wolf Creek Granola

¼ cup canola oil

1 cup maple syrup

¼ cup honey

½ teaspoon vanilla extract

1 tablespoon ground cinnamon

3 tablespoons fresh orange peel

2 tablespoons lemon juice concentrate

2 cups regular oatmeal

1 cup wheat germ

½ cup sweetened flaked coconut

½ cup chopped pecans

½ cup sunflower seed kernels

½ cup slivered almonds

½ cup dried cranberries

Water and powdered milk

Total weight: 2 pounds 7 ounces
Weight per serving: 5.5 ounces
Total servings: 7

At home:

In a covered saucepan, heat oil, maple syrup, and honey until boiling. Reduce heat to a very low, barely rolling boil. Add vanilla, cinnamon, and orange peel. Simmer for 15 minutes, then remove from heat and stir in the lemon juice concentrate. In a bowl, mix oatmeal, wheat germ, coconut, pecans, sunflower seeds, almonds, and dried cranberries. Pour in the syrup mix and stir well. After preheating the oven, spread the mixture onto two greased cookie sheets and bake at 275° for 30 minutes. Stir every 10 minutes or so, checking often to ensure that the granola doesn't burn. Divide into seven 1-cup servings and carry in resealable plastic bags.

For crunchier granola, add a little less honey and maple syrup and bake at 335°. For chewier granola, add a little more honey and/or maple syrup and bake at 320°.

On the trail:

Add water and powdered milk to your granola.

EMMETT AUTREY
"OL KOOGER"
AMARILLO, TEXAS

Nutritional information per serving

calories	630
protein	14 g
carbohydrates	86 g
sodium	20 mg
fiber	8 g
fat	23 g
cholesterol	0 mg

Lost Valley Granola

Total weight: 5 pounds 4 ounces
Weight per serving: 3.2 ounces
Total servings: 26 1-cup servings

At home:

Preheat oven to 300°. In a very large bowl, mix oats, coconut, buttermilk, All-Bran, brown sugar, wheat germ, sesame seeds, sunflower seeds, and almonds, stirring mixture after each addition. In a separate bowl, combine oil with vanilla and drizzle over oat mixture; stir thoroughly. Spread into four large baking pans and place in oven until coconut is golden brown. Stir frequently. May take as long as 2 hours to cook. Return mixture to large bowl. Add the raisins.

Cool and store in airtight containers. Packs well in resealable plastic bags for the trail.

On the trail:

Add powdered milk and water to 1 cup of granola or eat it right out of the bag.

ANN MARSHALL
PORT ORCHARD, WASHINGTON

10 cups rolled oats

4 cups flaked sweetened coconut

1 cup buttermilk

3 cups All-Bran

1 cup brown sugar

1 cup wheat germ

1 cup sesame seeds

2 cups sunflower seeds

1 cup almonds

$1\frac{1}{2}$ cups oil

1 teaspoon vanilla

3 cups raisins

Water and powdered milk (optional)

Nutritional information per serving

calories	550
protein	13 g
carbohydrates	62 g
sodium	80 mg
fiber	9 g
fat	31 g
cholesterol	3 mg

Gravel Road Granola

½ cup brown sugar

½ cup oil

½ cup honey

½ teaspoon vanilla

5½ cups oats

1½ cups chopped unsalted peanuts

1½ cups sweetened shredded coconut

1½ cups sunflower seeds

1 cup dried soybeans

2 cups chopped dried pears

Water and powdered milk

Total weight: 4 pounds
Weight per serving: 5 ounces
Total servings: 13 1-cup servings

At home:

Mix brown sugar, oil, honey, and vanilla. Using a hand mixer, blend with the dry ingredients. Spread on two oiled (or nonstick) cookie sheets. Bake at 325° for 15 minutes until brown. Turn mixture over every 3 to 5 minutes.

On the tráil:

Add powdered milk and water to 1 cup of granola.

DEBORAH BRILL
SCOTT "MARTY" PLACE
BERKELEY, CALIFORNIA

Don't sacrifice. Carry a little more food weight and eat well!

JEFFREY HARE
CITRUS HEIGHTS, CALIFORNIA

Nutritional information per serving

calories	610
protein	18 g
carbohydrates	51 g
sodium	50 mg
fiber	13 g
fat	34 g
cholesterol	0 mg

Cherry-Walnut Couscous Porridge

Total weight: 8 ounces
Weight per serving: 4 ounces
Total servings: 2

At home:
In a 1-gallon resealable plastic bag, combine all dry ingredients.

On the trail:
Bring water to a boil. Stir in dry mix, then cover and remove from heat. Allow to sit for 10 minutes. Stir and serve.

My sister-in-law, absolutely the best sister in-law, hunted up this recipe and made couscous porridge for me while I was on the trail in 1997. I found it to be nourishing, easy, and very tasty.

CATHY CZACHOROWSKI
TORRINGTON, CONNECTICUT

$\frac{1}{2}$ cup instant couscous

$\frac{1}{2}$ cup nonfat powdered milk

$\frac{1}{4}$ cup dried cherries (available at health food stores)

$\frac{1}{4}$ cup finely chopped walnuts

3 tablespoons light brown sugar

$\frac{1}{2}$ teaspoon ground cinnamon

$\frac{1}{8}$ teaspoon salt

$1\frac{1}{4}$ cups water

Nutritional information per serving

calories	460
protein	17 g
carbohydrates	80 g
sodium	240 mg
fiber	9 g
fat	9 g
cholesterol	3 mg

Mountain Corn Cakes

1 (7-ounce) package of corn bread mix

1 tablespoon powdered egg

2 tablespoons powdered milk

⅓ cup water (or just enough to make a spoonable batter)

1 tablespoon butter, margarine, or olive oil

Total weight: 8 ounces
Weight per serving: 4 ounces
Total servings: 2

At home:
Mix all dry ingredients and place in a resealable plastic bag.

On the trail:
Add water to the mix, seal the bag, and knead well by pressing and squeezing the bag. Melt butter in pan or skillet over a very low flame. Place large, heaping spoonfuls of the batter in your pan or skillet. The batter will spread some, so leave a little room between each or cook one at a time. When bubbles appear all over the surface, carefully flip cake onto the uncooked side. Cook another 30 to 40 seconds, or until the cake sounds hollow when lightly tapped. Repeat until all the batter is used. The cakes complement almost any food but are good by themselves as well.

I've made these in the morning and carried the leftovers wrapped in tissue paper in a fanny bag to eat as I walk or to have later for lunch.

CRAIG SMITH
"SMITTY"
SPRINGFIELD, MISSOURI

Nutritional information per serving

calories	450
protein	10 g
carbohydrates	3 g
sodium	860 mg
fiber	3 g
fat	15 g
cholesterol	55 mg

Cornmeal Mush

Total weight: 7 ounces
Weight per serving: 3.5 ounces
Total servings: 2

1 cup cornmeal

¼ teaspoon salt

2 tablespoons powdered buttermilk

2 tablespoons brown sugar

¼ teaspoon cinnamon

1 tablespoon butter per serving

¾ cup water per serving

At home:

In a resealable plastic bag, combine cornmeal, salt, powdered buttermilk, brown sugar, and cinnamon. To make individual meals, divide mixture into two sandwich-size resealable plastic bags. Carry butter separately.

On the trail:

Bring ¾ cup of water to a boil, add 1 tablespoon of butter, and slowly add one serving of cornmeal mush mix. Stir while heating for 1 minute. Take off heat and wrap entire pan in towel or other insulator for 3 to 5 minutes before eating.

IRWIN REEVES
BEAUMONT, CALIFORNIA

Authors' note
Don't let the name of this recipe turn you away. It is actually quite tasty!

Nutritional information per serving

calories	420
protein	8 g
carbohydrates	106 g
sodium	330 mg
fiber	2 g
fat	6 g
cholesterol	23 mg

Boulder Lake Breakfast Bars

2 cups quick oats

2 cups Health Valley Date and Almond Granola

1 cup raisins

⅓ cup brown sugar

¼ cup flour

½ cup margarine

½ cup light maple syrup

½ cup chunky peanut butter

1 cup semisweet chocolate chips

Total weight: 2 pounds
Weight per serving: 1 ounce (per 1-inch square)
Total servings: 32 bars

At home:

Mix oats, granola, raisins, brown sugar, and flour, using hands if necessary to break up any lumps in the raisins or granola. In a saucepan, melt margarine, then stir in maple syrup and peanut butter until blended. Stir the margarine mixture into the oats and mix well.

Turn mixture into oiled 9x13-inch pan and press firmly into place with greased fingers. Bake at 350° for 20 minutes. Remove from oven and sprinkle with chocolate chips. When chips melt (you may have to return the pan to the oven to help this happen), smooth out softened chocolate with a knife. When almost cool, cut into bars. Wrap in plastic and store until your trip. A couple of bars make a quick, no-cook breakfast.

In my search for a good homemade granola bar that I could use for a no-cook breakfast, I came across this one. It combines my two favorite foods: peanut butter and chocolate! The bars are very dense and filling, and a little goes a long way. They are great for mornings when you need to make a quick departure and don't have time to heat water for oatmeal.

ANN MARSHALL
PORT ORCHARD, WASHINGTON

I eat a breakfast bar or snack first thing in the morning so that I can get on the trail early. Beating the hot sun is a priority for me.

STEVE FUQUAY
"SWITCHBACK"
LAS VEGAS, NEVADA

Nutritional information per serving

calories	170
protein	3 g
carbohydrates	28 g
sodium	70 mg
fiber	2 g
fat	6 g
cholesterol	1 mg

Appalachian Apple Bannock

Total weight: 14 ounces
Weight per serving: 3.5 ounces
Total servings: 4

2 cups Bisquick

¼ cup dehydrated apple, cut into small pieces

2 tablespoons water per serving

1 tablespoon margarine per serving

Jam (optional)

At home:

Mix together Bisquick and dehydrated apple. To make separate servings, place ½ cup of mix into each of four sandwich-size resealable plastic bags. Carry margarine separately.

On the trail:

Add 2 tablespoons of water to one serving (one bag) of Bisquick and dehydrated apple mix, then mix and knead with hands until dough is slightly thinner than normal biscuit dough. Melt 1 tablespoon of butter in frying pan. Drop biscuit-size blobs into pan. Flatten slightly with spatula. Cook on low heat, turning once. Eat as is or with jam.

WALT AND JANE DANIELS
MOHEGAN LAKE, NEW YORK

Nutritional information per serving

calories	270
protein	3 g
carbohydrates	46 g
sodium	570 mg
fiber	1 g
fat	14 g
cholesterol	0 mg

"Scrambling Up the Sierra" Eggs

1½ cups powdered eggs (or powdered egg whites)

¼ teaspoon pepper (or to taste)

2 tablespoons dried bell pepper

1 tablespoon dried onion

4 teaspoons powdered buttermilk

1 teaspoon garlic powder

1½ cups water

1 tablespoon butter or oil

Total weight: 5 ounces
Weight per serving: 2.5 ounces
Total servings: 2

At home:

Mix eggs, pepper, bell pepper, onion, powdered buttermilk, and garlic and store in a resealable plastic bag.

On the trail:

Add water to the egg mixture and mix until the lumps disappear. Let sit for 5 to 10 minutes. Place butter in frying pan and heat over a low to medium flame. Pour eggs into pan and scramble.

Although we use powdered eggs in this recipe, fresh eggs can be cooked and dried at home, then rehydrated while on the trail.

TIM AND CHRISTINE CONNERS
CINCINNATI, OHIO

Nutritional information per serving

calories	330
protein	41 g
carbohydrates	16 g
sodium	710 mg
fiber	0 g
fat	7 g
cholesterol	25 mg

Kitchen Creek Breakfast Rice

Total weight: 10 ounces
Total servings: 1

At home:
In a large resealable plastic bag, combine rice, raisins, pecans, sugar, and cinnamon. Carry salt separately.

On the trail:
Bring water and salt to a boil. Add remainder of ingredients, then cover and simmer 10 minutes until rice is tender.

Ursula Brower
South Lake Tahoe, California

1 cup instant brown rice

¼ cup raisins (or any dried fruit)

¼ cup chopped pecans

2 tablespoons sugar

1 teaspoon cinnamon

(Other seasonings can be added such as brown sugar, butter, dried milk, or whatever you can scrape off the bottom of your pack!)

¼ teaspoon salt

1¼ cups water

I love my pack oven. I don't bake very much with it, as mixes can be heavy. However, I do use it to cook most of my meals. As a result, I almost never have to wash dishes, and I never burn food. I have improved my level of cooking sanitation and am able to easily cook unprocessed rice, which is healthier, cheaper, and better tasting.

Will O'Daix
"The Green Ghost"
Indianapolis, Indiana

Nutritional information per serving

calories	800
protein	11 g
carbohydrates	148 g
sodium	620 mg
fiber	6 g
fat	18 g
cholesterol	0 mg

Chicken Curry Salad

Salad:

5 cups cooked brown rice

½ cup white wine vinegar

4 (5-ounce) cans low-fat chicken

1 cup finely chopped celery

1 cup finely chopped carrots

1 cup finely chopped apples

½ cup minced parsley

½ cup minced green pepper

2 tablespoons minced dried onion

½ cup sunflower seeds

Dressing:

4 tablespoons olive oil

4 tablespoons safflower oil

2 teaspoons brown sugar

½ teaspoon salt

1 teaspoon garlic powder

2 teaspoons curry powder

1 teaspoon cumin powder

¾ cup water per serving

Total weight with dressing: 1 pound 8 ounces
Weight for dressing only: 4 ounces
Weight per serving (with dressing): 4 ounces
Total servings: 6

At home:

Salad: In a large bowl, toss the cooked brown rice with the vinegar, set aside, and allow to soak for ½ hour. Add chicken (broken up into small pieces), celery, carrots, apple, parsley, green pepper, onion, and sunflower seeds. On six separate plastic-lined drying trays (each tray equals one serving), place 1¾ cups of rice mixture and dehydrate. When completely dry, place each serving in a separate resealable plastic bag.

Dressing: In a separate bowl, combine olive oil, safflower oil, brown sugar, salt, garlic powder, curry powder, and cumin powder. Place in a leakproof squeeze bottle.

On the trail:

The night before you plan to eat this meal, place ¾ cup of water into one bag (one serving) of salad mix. Keep salad at the bottom of the bag and roll up the bag like a burrito to help keep it from leaking. Allow to sit overnight. In the morning, check how the rehydration is progressing and, if necessary, add more water. The salad should be fully rehydrated by lunchtime. At lunchtime, stir a sixth of your seasoned oil into one serving of salad.

Because of these salad recipes, our backpacking buddies were vying to share our meals. Every evening before the next day's hike, I would toss the salad ingredients in a leakproof Tupperware container, add plenty of filtered water, seal the container, and stow the lunch away in a pack along with spoons and seasoned oil. As we trudged along the next day, each yummy morsel was reabsorbing the water removed days prior. By lunchtime, a succulent and hearty salad would be ready with a liberal application of seasoned oil. Our food group would select a "table" with a view and nourish our bodies and spirits.

Nutritional information per serving

calories	610
protein	30 g
carbohydrates	54 g
sodium	600 mg
fiber	6 g
fat	29 g
cholesterol	59 mg

PAM COZ-HILL
VISALIA, CALIFORNIA

Creamy Cilantro Tuna Salad

Total weight with dressing: 1 pound 6 ounces
Weight for dressing only: 6 ounces
Weight per serving (with dressing): 5.5 ounces
Total servings: 4

At home:

Salad: Cook pasta, rinse, and drain. Place macaroni in large bowl and toss with cabbage, celery, cucumber, radishes, cilantro, green onion, tuna, and walnuts. To dry, place salad on four separate drying trays (one tray per serving, 3 cups of salad per tray). When fully dehydrated, place the contents of each tray into one resealable plastic bag.

Dressing: Combine oil, vinegar, garlic, mustard, brown sugar, and salt. Pour into leakproof squeeze bottle and refrigerate until departing for the trail. Carry mayonnaise packets separately.

On the trail:

The evening before you plan to have the salad for lunch, add 1 cup of water to a serving of salad in its resealable plastic bag. In the morning, check to see how the rehydration is progressing and, if necessary, add more water. At lunchtime, add a fourth of the dressing to each serving as well as the contents of one mayonnaise packet. Pass out the spoons, because everyone will want to have some!

PAM COZ-HILL
VISALIA, CALIFORNIA

Salad:
- 1 (16-ounce) bag pasta salad
- 1½ cups finely shredded green cabbage
- 1 cup chopped celery
- ½ cup chopped cucumber
- ½ cup sliced radishes
- ½ cup packed, minced fresh cilantro (or coriander leaves)
- ½ cup chopped green onion
- 1 (6-ounce) can water-packed tuna, drained
- ¾ cup chopped walnuts
- 1 cup water per serving to rehydrate the salad on the trail

Dressing:
- ¼ cup safflower oil
- 4 tablespoons white wine vinegar
- 1 teaspoon garlic powder
- 4 teaspoons Dijon mustard
- 2 teaspoons brown sugar
- 1 teaspoon salt
- 4 single-serving packets of mayonnaise

Nutritional information per serving

calories	870
protein	29 g
carbohydrates	92 g
sodium	970 mg
fiber	7 g
fat	46 g
cholesterol	21 mg

Sierra Szechwan Chicken Salad

½ cup soy sauce

½ teaspoon Szechwan chili oil

1 teaspoon Dijon mustard

1 pound thin somen (Japanese noodles) or capellini

4 quarts boiling water

2 (5-ounce) cans light chicken meat

6 green onions, thinly sliced

1 red sweet pepper, coarsely chopped

1 green bell pepper, coarsely chopped

2 carrots, peeled and thinly sliced crossways

1 (8-ounce) can sliced bamboo shoots, drained

1 (15-ounce) can miniature corn on the cob, drained and thinly sliced

8 ounces petite frozen peas

1 tablespoon dried cilantro

2 tablespoons lightly toasted sesame seeds

Sesame seed oil (optional)

¾ cup water per serving

Nutritional information per serving

calories	380
protein	19 g
carbohydrates	62 g
sodium	3,110 mg
fiber	5 g
fat	6 g
cholesterol	29 mg

Total weight: 1 pound 2 ounces
Weight per serving: 3 ounces
Total servings: 6

At home:

Mix soy sauce, chili oil, and mustard in a large bowl. Cook noodles (somen) in the boiling water until al dente. Drain and toss the noodles in the soy sauce-chili oil-mustard mix, making sure to coat the noodles thoroughly. Spread out thinly on the drying tray and dehydrate. Also dehydrate the chicken, green onions, red and green peppers, carrots, bamboo shoots, corn, and peas.

When dried, break the noodles into 1-inch-long pieces and toss them in a large bowl with the rest of the dried ingredients. Add the dried cilantro and sesame seeds. Divide mixture into six 3-ounce portions. Each portion will represent one serving. Store each serving in a 1-gallon resealable plastic bag.

On the trail:

The night before you are ready to eat this meal for lunch, add ¾ cup of water to each serving of the noodle mixture. Allow to sit overnight. Periodically toss the water around in the bag. In the morning, check to see how the rehydration is progressing and, if necessary, add more water. By lunchtime the meal should be completely rehydrated. You can eat it at room temperature, allow it to chill a few minutes in a cold river, or heat it briefly over a stove.

PAM COZ-HILL
VISALIA, CALIFORNIA

Authors' note
Sodium content can be reduced by using low-sodium soy sauce.

Tropical Trail Salad

Total weight: 1 pound 4 ounces
Weight per serving: 5 ounces
Total servings: 4

At home:

Bring water to a boil. Add rice. Let simmer for 5 minutes or until water is absorbed and rice is tender. Toss the brown rice in a large bowl with the lemon juice and coconut milk. Set aside for ½ hour to soak. Add the rest of the ingredients and mix. Place 2¼ cups of rice mixture on each of four separate drying trays (one tray per serving). Dry and package each serving in a resealable plastic bag.

On the trail:

In the morning, before hitting the trail, add 1 cup of water to a single-serving bag of rice mix. Be sure it is sealed well. By lunchtime, you will have a delicious tropical trail salad waiting for you.

PAM COZ-HILL
VISALIA, CALIFORNIA

2½ cups water

2½ cups Brown Minute Rice

½ cup lemon juice

½ cup coconut milk

1 carrot, coarsely grated

1 apple, coarsely grated

2 stalks celery, thinly sliced

1 cup shredded cabbage

1 cup chopped dried apricot (or your favorite dried fruit)

½ cup chopped dates (or your favorite dried fruit)

¼ cup toasted almonds

1 tablespoon dried parsley flakes

1½ teaspoons salt

¼ cup honey

1 cup water per serving to rehydrate

Nutritional information per serving

calories	580
protein	11 g
carbohydrates	108 g
sodium	930 mg
fiber	8 g
fat	17 g
cholesterol	0 mg

Hudson Bay Bread

16 tablespoons (2 sticks) butter (or margarine)

1½ cups sugar

6 cups rolled oats

⅔ cup honey

½ cup raisins

½ cup peanuts

Total weight: 3 pounds
Weight per serving: 1.5 ounces
Total servings: 32 (1 bar per serving)

At home:

In a large pan, melt butter. Add sugar and stir. Add 3 cups of the oats and stir. Heat the honey in a microwave until it becomes a runny liquid (about 30 seconds), then add it to the bowl along with the raisins, peanuts, and the rest of the oats. Mix by hand. Place in an ungreased baking pan (15¼x10¼ x¾-inch). Bake at 350º until golden brown (about 25 to 30 minutes).

Important: Allow to cool 10 minutes before cutting. After cutting, allow to cool another 10 minutes, and then flip out of the pan. Let the bread cool completely before wrapping.

My favorite food on the Pacific Crest Trail was Hudson Bay Bread. It must have been my favorite, because it was always the first thing I ate when I'd pick up my food at every post office resupply drop.

When I was a Boy Scout, my troop would go to the Northern Wisconsin National Canoe Base, operated by the Boy Scouts of America in Boulder Junction, Wisconsin. Before heading out, the base would provide us with provisions, including Hudson Bay Bread made in their own kitchens, along with lots of peanut butter and honey. Even my brother liked it, and he doesn't like much. Happy Trails!

ALAN YOUNG
SCOTTSDALE, ARIZONA

Authors' note

Though it tastes more like a sweet snack than a bread, Hudson Bay Bread has a history of use as a staple and is thus included in the "Lunch" section. It's delicious.

Nutritional information per serving

calories	220
protein	4 g
carbohydrates	19 g
sodium	90 mg
fiber	3 g
fat	13 g
cholesterol	0 mg

Smitty's Lunch at Lost Lake

Total weight (including sardine tin): 10 ounces
Weight per serving: 5 ounces
Total servings: 2 (6 crackers per serving)

3 prewrapped slices of
   American cheese

12 Triscuits

1 4.2-ounce tin of sardines

On the trail:

Fold each piece of cheese in half twice. On each cracker, place a piece of cheese, then a bit of sardine.

Most of the time, I like really simple lunches. My brother and I first had this lunch at Lost Lake, about four miles from the trailhead in the Beartooth Mountains. The lake is quite small and is faced on the south by impressive rock buttresses. The winds that day were about fifty miles an hour. We've also eaten this while sitting on the bluffs along the Buffalo River in northwest Arkansas.

CRAIG SMITH
"SMITTY"
SPRINGFIELD, MISSOURI

Authors' note

Smitty's original recipe called for Ritz crackers, which don't hold up as well as Triscuits in the pack. Triscuits also have more fiber. However, the recipe is simple, so use your favorite cracker or your favorite type of cheese.

Nutritional information per serving

calories	320
protein	19 g
carbohydrates	21 g
sodium	1,950 mg
fiber	4 g
fat	19 g
cholesterol	83 mg

Backpacker's Snack Attack Bars

6 ounces frozen orange juice concentrate, thawed and undiluted

$\frac{1}{2}$ cup uncooked quick oats

$\frac{1}{2}$ cup chopped pitted prunes

$\frac{1}{2}$ cup chopped dried apricots

$\frac{1}{2}$ cup raisins

$\frac{1}{2}$ cup chopped unsalted peanuts

$\frac{1}{4}$ cup chopped dates

$\frac{1}{4}$ cup wheat germ

$\frac{1}{4}$ cup sesame seeds

1 tablespoon shortening

$\frac{1}{2}$ cup sugar

$\frac{1}{2}$ cup unsulphured molasses

1 egg

2 cups sifted all-purpose flour

$\frac{1}{4}$ teaspoon salt

1 teaspoon baking soda

1 teaspoon ginger

1 teaspoon cinnamon

Courtesy The Daily Gazette *(Schenectady, NY)*

Total weight: 2 pounds 6 ounces
Weight per serving: 1.1 ounces
Total servings: 36 (1 bar per serving)

At home:

In a large bowl, mix concentrate, oats, prunes, apricots, raisins, peanuts, dates, wheat germ, and sesame seeds. In a separate bowl, blend shortening and sugar with a hand mixer (if difficult, soften in microwave for a few seconds). To the second bowl add the molasses and egg and mix well. In a third bowl combine sifted flour, salt, baking soda, ginger, and cinnamon; add to molasses mixture, stir, then add the fruit mixture and stir again. Pour into greased 13x9x2-inch baking pan and spread evenly. Bake in oven at 325º for 35 minutes. Cool and cut into 3x1-inch bars. Wrap in plastic or foil for the trail.

This recipe was adapted with permission from an article about backpacking published in the Schenectady *Gazette* more than 20 years ago.

DAVID AND SANDRA GEISINGER
SCHENECTADY, NEW YORK

Authors' note
This recipe is good as a snack, as the name implies, but its long list of wholesome ingredients also makes it suitable as a lunch staple. This recipe is suitable for drying.

Nutritional information per serving

calories	112
protein	3 g
carbohydrates	19 g
sodium	60 mg
fiber	1 g
fat	4 g
cholesterol	4 mg

White Mountain Tortillas

Total weight: 1 pound 4 ounces
Weight per serving: 10 ounces
Total servings: 2 (2 tortillas per serving)

At home:
Package each item separately.

On the trail:
Mix hummus with water. For each tortilla, heat 1 tablespoon of oil in pan. Place a fourth of the hummus on top of one tortilla, and place one slice of cheese on top of the hummus. Place tortilla in heated pan. Cover pan and cook until cheese has melted. Do the same to make the remaining three tortillas.

Variations: Try using sprouts instead of cheese. To reduce weight, substitute Parmesan cheese for provolone.

WALT AND JANE DANIELS
MOHEGAN LAKE, NEW YORK

1 package Fantastic Foods Hummus

1½ cups water

4 slices provolone cheese

4 reduced-fat whole-wheat tortillas

4 tablespoons olive oil (or other oil)

Nutritional information per serving

calories	1,030
protein	47 g
carbohydrates	103 g
sodium	2,710 mg
fiber	15 g
fat	52 g
cholesterol	70 mg

Trekker's Tabouli on Pita

1 fresh zucchini

1 fresh bell pepper

1 6-ounce box Fantastic Tabouli

2 tablespoons minced dried onion

1 tablespoon dried oregano leaves

1 tablespoon dried basil leaves

2 bay (laurel) leaves, crumbled

1 teaspoon dried sage

1 teaspoon dried parsley

1 tablespoon nutritional yeast

1⅓ cups water (⅓ cup per serving)

4 tablespoons olive oil (1 tablespoon per serving)

4 slices Kraft Deluxe Swiss Cheese (1 slice per serving)

4 whole-wheat pitas (1 pita per serving)

Total weight: 1 pound 4 ounces
Weight per serving: 5 ounces
Total servings: 4 (1 pita per serving)

At home:

Finely chop zucchini and bell pepper and dry in a food dehydrator. In a large bowl, mix together zucchini, bell pepper, tabouli, minced onion, oregano, basil, bay leaves, sage, parsley, and nutritional yeast. To make four individual servings, divide tabouli mixture into four 2-ounce portions. Each serving will require 1 pita, 1 slice of cheese, and 1 tablespoon of oil, all of which you store separately in your pack.

On the trail:

To one bag of tabouli mixture, add ⅓ cup of water and 1 tablespoon of olive oil. Allow to sit for about 2 hours while hiking. To serve, place 1 piece of cheese in one sliced pita. Cut a large hole in the bottom of the tabouli bag and squirt the tabouli into the pita. No cooking is necessary.

This meal is nutritious and great on the trail because it does not require cooking and messy pots and pans.

SANDY LEE BURNS
PROSPECT, OREGON

Nutritional information per serving

calories	540
protein	21 g
carbohydrates	65 g
sodium	1,250 mg
fiber	8 g
fat	26 g
cholesterol	25 mg

BMCS

Total weight: 11 ounces
Weight per serving: 5.5 ounces
Total servings: 2

At home:
Place each item in a separate bag for the trail.

On the trail:
This one's easy. Layer your meat and cheese on the bottom half of one split bagel. Place the top half of the bagel where it naturally goes and eat. It's very filling. Pepperoni and pepper jack cheese work very well also. For zing, carry some individual packets of regular or hot mustard and squirt them on. For variety, try different types of bagels, meats, and cheeses.

My brother and I first made these BMCs (Bagel, Meat, and Cheese sandwiches) at a small lake in the Wind River Range that had the most incredible trout fishing I've ever experienced. "Which lake?" you ask. I'm not telling.

CRAIG SMITH
"SMITTY"
SPRINGFIELD, MISSOURI

2 onion bagels, split

2 ounces summer sausage (or dried chipped beef or pepperoni)

2 ounces sharp cheddar cheese (or American or Swiss cheese)

Nutritional information per serving

calories	480
protein	43 g
carbohydrates	53 g
sodium	1,480 mg
fiber	3 g
fat	49 g
cholesterol	139 mg

Tuna-Spinach Couscous

1 (6-ounce) can tuna, packed in water

1 cup couscous

1 (1.8-ounce) package Knorr Cream of Spinach Dried Soup Mix

3 tablespoons powdered buttermilk

1 cup water per serving

Total weight: 11 ounces
Weight per serving: 5.5 ounces
Total servings: 2

At home:

Dry tuna in food dehydrator. Mix all dry ingredients together and divide evenly into two separate resealable plastic bags.

On the trail:

Add 1 cup water to one serving of couscous. Mush around a bit, then let sit for 1 hour before eating.

DIANE KING
SOMERS, CONNECTICUT

Learn the joys of couscous! It is high in protein, needs no straining, and takes less time to cook than pasta but can be used in all the same ways.

DAN AND SARA RUFNER
SAN DIEGO, CALIFORNIA

Nutritional information per serving

calories	600
protein	35 g
carbohydrates	89 g
sodium	1,440 mg
fiber	4 g
fat	12 g
cholesterol	39 mg

Oak Creek Cheese Cookies

Total weight: 1 pound 1 ounce
Weight per serving: 0.5 ounce
Total servings: 36 (1 cookie per serving)

1 cup whole-wheat flour

$\frac{1}{2}$ cup (1 stick) butter, softened

1 cup grated cheddar cheese

$\frac{1}{2}$ cup soft cream cheese

$\frac{1}{4}$ cup pecans

$\frac{1}{4}$ cup flax seed

$\frac{1}{8}$ teaspoon cayenne

At home:

Preheat oven to 350°. Mix flour and butter. Add cheddar cheese, cream cheese, pecans, flax seed, and cayenne. Mix again. Roll into 36 balls and flatten on a large cookie sheet, in the manner that you would make homemade cookies. Cook for 9 minutes at 350°. When finished baking, let cool, then package in plastic bags.

The Pacific Crest Trail runs above the Oak Creek Canyon south of the town of Tehachapi, California. It's a beautiful area, an oasis surrounded by desert. In fact, wild horses still run the canyon floor. We often hiked the trails near here.

Tim and Christine Conners
Cincinnati, Ohio

Nutritional information per serving

calories	70
protein	2 g
carbohydrates	5 g
sodium	50 mg
fiber	0 g
fat	6 g
cholesterol	14 mg

Peanut Butter and Raisin Roll-ups

2 tablespoons peanut butter

2 tablespoons (1 ounce) raisins

2 medium flour tortillas

Total weight: 8 ounces
Total servings: 1

At home:
Store all ingredients separately in your pack.

On the trail:
Spread half the peanut butter on each tortilla. Add raisins to each. Roll up and eat. It's simple, requires no cooking or cleanup, and is very tasty.

KEVIN CORCORAN
PALMDALE, CALIFORNIA

Authors' note
As a variant, try honey instead of raisins. Peanut butter and honey roll-ups are energy storehouses.

Nutritional information per serving

calories	750
protein	36 g
carbohydrates	100 g
sodium	810 mg
fiber	8 g
fat	31 g
cholesterol	0 mg

Simmering Pot Fruit Soup

Total weight: 1 pound 4 ounces
Weight per serving: 10 ounces
Total servings: 2

At home:
Pack all fruit together in a plastic bag and carry pudding mix separately.

On the trail:
Bring fruit to a boil in pot with 3 cups of water and simmer for 10 minutes (longer if you can spare the fuel). Turn off heat. Mix 1 cup water with lemon pudding in a plastic bottle until dissolved. Mix with fruit soup and serve in cups.

SANDY LEE BURNS
PROSPECT, OREGON

1 pound Sun Sweet Dried Fruit Bits (or 5 dried pieces of each of the following cut into 1-inch squares: pears, apples, pineapple rings, papaya, peaches, apricot, prunes, or dates)

1 (3.4-ounce) package instant lemon pudding

3 cups water (to rehydrate fruit)

1 cup water (for pudding)

Nutritional information per serving

calories	780
protein	8 g
carbohydrates	208 g
sodium	800 mg
fiber	1 g
fat	0 g
cholesterol	0 mg

Domeland Nachos

2 medium flour tortillas

3-ounce chunk of sharp cheddar cheese

2 tablespoons oil per tortilla

Total weight: 11 ounces
Weight per serving: 5.5 ounces
Total servings: 2

At home:
Store all ingredients separately.

On the trail:
For each serving, cut one tortilla into pie slices. Cut cheese into thin flat pieces. Heat 2 tablespoons of oil in frying pan. Place slices from 1 tortilla in pan with hot oil. Allow one side to cook, and then flip. Drop pieces of cheese onto tortillas and cover pan, if possible. Heat on low until cheese melts. Cook other tortilla the same way.

I got bit by the backpacking bug when I was 27 years old while on a day hike in the Domeland Wilderness of the Southern Sierra. I remember not wanting to go initially; but, thankfully, a persistent coworker convinced me it would be worth the effort. Once we arrived at the trailhead, I was completely mesmerized by the beauty and solitude of the region. At the end of the day, I couldn't wait to return there with a backpack to spend a few nights on the trail. The following month, I did just that. Inexperienced and improperly equipped for November mountain weather, I headed into the wilderness. Several days later, in the middle of the night, I limped back out, injured and exhausted but with a love of the mountains and the trail that hasn't faded.

—Tim

TIM AND CHRISTINE CONNERS
CINCINNATI, OHIO

Nutritional information per serving

calories	700
protein	16 g
carbohydrates	37 g
sodium	610 mg
fiber	2 g
fat	57 g
cholesterol	15 mg

Wagon Mound Tortilla Chips

Total weight: 8 ounces
Weight per serving: 4 ounces
Total servings: 2

5 tablespoons oil
2 medium tortillas
1 teaspoon salt

At home:
Store all ingredients separately.

On the trail:
Heat oil in frying pan. Cut tortillas into pie slices. Place slices in hot oil. Fry until light brown and crispy on one side, then turn over and repeat on opposite side. Be careful not to burn the tortillas! Add salt when both sides are finished cooking. At this point, having dehydrated salsa in your pack will make you the envy of your camp.

TIM AND CHRISTINE CONNERS
CINCINNATI, OHIO

We recently switched from pita bread to tortillas as our bread source. The tortillas hold up better on the trail, are lighter, and make great peanut butter and jelly, cheese, or tuna roll-up sandwiches.

JOE AND CLAIRE HAGEMAN
TRENTON, NORTH CAROLINA

Nutritional information per serving

calories	530
protein	5 g
carbohydrates	36 g
sodium	1,500 mg
fiber	2 g
fat	43 g
cholesterol	0 mg

Matt Food

2 cups peanut butter

2 cups low-fat powdered milk

½ cup honey

1 cup rolled oats

Nuts, coconut, dried fruit, cinnamon, wheat germ, vanilla (optional)

Total weight: 2 pounds
Weight per serving: 1 ounce
Total servings: 32

At home:
Mix all of the ingredients together. This recipe can be stored in a container and used like peanut butter or rolled into two 16-ounce logs and cut into slices when you're ready to eat it.

Matt Food is great plain, or with crackers, bread, chocolate, or in oatmeal.

Deborah Brill
Scott "Marty" Place
Berkeley, California

Try new recipes and cooking methods in your backyard before you begin your adventure in the wilderness.

Jeffrey Hare
Citrus Heights, California

Nutritional information per serving

calories	140
protein	6 g
carbohydrates	10 g
sodium	90 mg
fiber	1 g
fat	8 g
cholesterol	2 mg

Hawk Mountain Roll-ups

Total weight: 5 ounces
Total servings: 1

At home:
Pack all ingredients separately.

On the trail:
Add black bean mix to water. Let sit a few minutes until bean mix is fully rehydrated. Grate or chop cheese. Spread bean dip on a tortilla with cheese and roll it up.

WALT AND JANE DANIELS
MOHEGAN LAKE, NEW YORK

1 envelope dried
    McCormick Collection
    Black Bean Mix

½ cup water

1 ounce cheddar cheese

1 medium wheat tortilla

Nutritional information per serving

calories	460
protein	17 g
carbohydrates	44 g
sodium	1,310 mg
fiber	8 g
fat	14 g
cholesterol	29 mg

Wild Turkey Jerky

2 pounds cooked lean
    turkey breast

Marinade:

1 teaspoon salt

1 teaspoon pepper

3 teaspoons brown sugar

¼ cup Worcestershire
    Sauce

¼ cup soy sauce

1 teaspoon liquid smoke

Total weight: 12 ounces
Weight per serving: 1 ounce
Total servings: 12

At home:

Partially freeze the meat to facilitate slicing. Cut thin slices (between ¹⁄₁₆- and ⅛-inch thick) across the grain of the meat. If you desire a chewier texture for the jerky, slice the meat with the grain.

Mix all marinade ingredients in a bowl, then layer meat in a plastic container and pour marinade over sliced meat, making sure to wet all surfaces. Cover container tightly and allow to sit in the refrigerator overnight. Invert container occasionally to keep meat moistened with the marinade.

Remove meat from container and place in a single layer, either on drying trays or on cookie cooling racks placed on cookie sheets. Place the meat in the oven and dry at 145° for 4 hours. Then reduce oven temperature to 130° until meat is thoroughly dry. Do not open the oven door too often or the meat may not dry properly.

Jerky should be hard but not brittle. Blot up any extra fat with paper towels.

BOB BALLOU
SACRAMENTO, CALIFORNIA

Nutritional information per serving

calories	100
protein	18 g
carbohydrates	2 g
sodium	1,150 mg
fiber	0 g
fat	1 g
cholesterol	23 mg

California Beef Jerky

Total weight: 10 ounces
Weight per serving: 2 ounces
Total servings: 5

At home:
Trim fat off steak and cut lengthwise along the grain no more than ½-inch thick. Cover with soy sauce. Arrange beef strips in a single layer on a wire rack placed on a baking sheet. Sprinkle with garlic salt and lemon pepper. Place a second rack over beef and flip over. Remove the top rack. Sprinkle again with seasoning. Bake at 175° overnight (about 10 to 12 hours). Pat meat strips with paper towels to remove any oil. Store in a covered container. Take on the trail sealed in a container or bag.

PEG SPRY
AGUA DULCE, CALIFORNIA

Authors' note:
Sodium content can be reduced by using low sodium soy sauce.

1½ pounds well-trimmed flank steak

½ cup soy sauce

2 tablespoons garlic salt

2 tablespoons lemon pepper

Nutritional information per serving

calories	220
protein	28 g
carbohydrates	1 g
sodium	2,620 mg
fiber	0 g
fat	10 g
cholesterol	66 mg

Appalachian Trail Jerky

2 pounds flank steak

Marinade:

⅓ cup teriyaki sauce

2 tablespoons liquid smoke

¼ cup low-salt soy sauce

2 tablespoons Worcestershire Sauce

1 tablespoon garlic powder

½ teaspoon onion powder

2 teaspoons pepper

2 teaspoons crushed red pepper

2 tablespoons brown sugar

Total weight: 12 ounces
Weight per serving: 1 ounce
Total servings: 12

At home:
Trim fat from steak and slice with grain into ¼x1½-inch strips. Combine marinade ingredients in a bowl. Add beef strips and stir, making sure sauce covers meat. Cover with plastic and marinate overnight. The next day, place meat strips flat on two large cookie sheets. Bake in a 150° oven for about 10 to 12 hours. Pack in a sealed container or bag.

We recently completed a stretch in the 100 Mile Wilderness. While on the trek, we enjoyed Appalachian Trail Jerky both as a staple food and as a bite on the go.

MARK AND JEN WATSON
"DOC AND THUMPER"
MECHANIC FALLS, MAINE

Nutritional information per serving

calories	200
protein	22 g
carbohydrates	4 g
sodium	530 mg
fiber	0 g
fat	10 g
cholesterol	54 mg

Heat Seeker's Gorp

Total weight: 6 pounds 5 ounces
Weight per serving: 3.9 ounces
Total servings: 26 (1 cup per serving)

At home:
Mix ingredients together and package in resealable plastic bags for the trail.

<small>GARY ADAMS
"DOCTARI"
CINCINNATI, OHIO</small>

Authors' note
Don't waste your time looking for Hot Bits at your local grocery store. They are small, hot, spice-covered crackers that can only be ordered from Supreme Nut and Candy Company, 6157 Glenway Avenue, Cincinnati, Ohio, 45211; (513) 662-1055. They pack a punch and are rather durable. If you can find something similar in your local grocery, great. If not, give Hot Bits a try.

1 pound Hot Bits (see Authors' note)

2½ pounds raisins

1 pound unsalted pepitas

½ pound dry-roasted salted peanuts

½ pound dry-roasted unsalted cashews

½ pound unsalted sunflower seeds

½ pound hot and spicy peanuts

Nutritional information per serving

calories	480
protein	12 g
carbohydrates	61 g
sodium	200 mg
fiber	14 g
fat	24 g
cholesterol	0 mg

Green Mountain Fruit Gorp

1 cup hazelnuts

1 cup walnuts

1 cup pumpkin seeds,
   roasted and salted

1 cup dried papaya, cut
   into bite-size pieces

1 cup dried pineapple, cut
   into bite-size pieces

1 cup dried figs, cut into
   bite-size pieces

1 cup dried prunes

Total weight: 2 pounds
Weight per serving: 4.6 ounces
Total servings: 7 (1 cup per serving)

At home:
Mix ingredients together. Place into 1 large resealable plastic bag or divide into seven servings of 1 cup each.

ALLMUTH PERZEL
"CURLY"
TOLLAND, CONNECTICUT

Authors' note
We've included all of our gorp recipes in the "Lunch" section because many trekkers eat nothing but gorp during their midday break. Besides, most folks view it more as a staple and less as a candy or treat. As an aside, ever wonder where the name "gorp" comes from? It's an acronym for "good old raisins and peanuts." As you can see, the gorp recipes in this section take it a few steps further.

Nutritional information per serving

calories	470
protein	13 g
carbohydrates	44 g
sodium	10 mg
fiber	7 g
fat	28 g
cholesterol	0 mg

Goose's Gorp

Total weight: 3 pounds 8 ounces
Weight per serving: 4.7 ounces
Total servings: 12 (1 cup per serving)

At home:

Mix all ingredients together and store in resealable plastic bags. One cup is equal to one serving.

KATHLEEN CUTSHALL
"THE OLD GRAY GOOSE"
CONNEAUT, OHIO

2 cups gumdrops

2 cups plain M&M's

$\frac{1}{2}$ cup roasted and salted pepitas (available at health food stores)

$\frac{1}{2}$ cup roasted and salted peanuts

2 (8-ounce) bags Sun Maid Mixed Fruit (or 2 cups of your favorite mix)

$\frac{1}{2}$ cup roasted and salted sunflower seeds

4 cups Honey Nut Cheerios

$\frac{1}{2}$ cup raisins

Shredded coconut (optional)

Nutritional information per serving

calories	450
protein	7 g
carbohydrates	87 g
sodium	240 mg
fiber	7 g
fat	13 g
cholesterol	4 mg

Sky Lakes Gorp

½ cup vegetable oil

¼ cup Worcestershire Sauce

2 teaspoons garlic salt

2 tablespoons barbecue sauce

1 box Mini Wheats

½ cup wheat germ

2 cups mini pretzels

2 cups Cheese Nips

2 cups honey-roasted peanuts

2 cups Cheerios

Total weight: 2 pounds 8 ounces
Weight per serving: 2.9 ounces
Total servings: 14 (1 cup per serving)

At home:

Preheat oven to 350º. In a large bowl, mix together vegetable oil, Worcestershire Sauce, garlic salt, barbecue sauce, Mini Wheats, and wheat germ. Spread on cookie sheet. Bake for 15 minutes or until browned. Return to large bowl and add pretzels, Cheese Nips, peanuts, and Cheerios. Store in resealable plastic bags to keep fresh.

On the trail:

Eat straight out of the bag or enjoy with peanut butter on a pita or tortilla for lunch.

ALYSSA PINKERTON AND JEAN CAPELLARI
ALLEN PARK, MICHIGAN

Nutritional information per serving

calories	380
protein	11 g
carbohydrates	50 g
sodium	450 mg
fiber	6 g
fat	13 g
cholesterol	1 mg

Bombaci's Tasty Trail Gorp

Total weight: 2 pounds 8 ounces
Weight per serving: 5 ounces
Total servings: 8 (1 cup per serving)

At home:
Mix all ingredients together and bag gorp for the trail.

RICK BOMBACI
ENTERPRISE, OREGON

1 cup unsalted cashews

1 cup unsalted sunflower seeds

1 cup sweetened shredded coconut

1 cup banana chips

1 cup raisins

1 cup chocolate chips

1 cup unsalted peanuts

1 cup dates

Nutritional information per serving

calories	660
protein	14 g
carbohydrates	96 g
sodium	70 mg
fiber	8 g
fat	36 g
cholesterol	4 mg

Dinner

Trail Oven Pizza to Go

1 package Boboli Pizza Sauce

1 package cheese mix from a box of Kraft Macaroni and Cheese

1 (6-ounce) package Chef Boyardee Pizza Crust Mix

½ cup water to add to sauce-cheese mix

1 tablespoon oil

½ cup warm water to add to crust mix

Topping ideas include

Dehydrated mushrooms

Dehydrated tomatoes

Pepperoni

Dehydrated bell peppers

Dehydrated onions

Spam

Sardines

Dehydrated zucchini

Dehydrated pineapple

Beef jerky

Almost anything leftover in your pack

Nutritional information per serving:
(does not include the extra toppings)

calories	880
protein	42 g
carbohydrates	33 g
sodium	3,640 mg
fiber	6 g
fat	28 g
cholesterol	30 mg

Total weight (without extra toppings): 9 ounces
Total servings: 1 (2 small pizzas)

At home:
Dry Boboli sauce on plastic wrap in a food dehydrator. Once dry, tear into small pieces. Mix dried Boboli sauce pieces together with cheese mix and store in a sandwich-size resealable plastic bag. Any dried vegetables for use as topping can be carried together with the sauce mix. Pour pizza crust mix into another sandwich-size resealable plastic bag. Pack oil separately. Remember to bring a pack oven!

On the trail:
Place water in sauce bag, adding more if you have dehydrated vegetables. Knead contents of bag until reconstituted, about 10 minutes for sauce, up to 1 hour if you have added vegetables. Place ½ cup of warm water in pizza crust bag along with 1 tablespoon of oil. Knead for at least 1 minute. Allow dough to rise in bag for 5 minutes in a warm place. (If you are in a cold environment, stick the bag in a warm place inside your jacket.)

At this point, follow the directions specific to the type of backpacking oven you are using, but basically the pizza dough goes on the bottom of the baking tray, and the sauce, as you might expect, goes on top of the dough. If your oven requires a bag, you may choose to fold your dough over your sauce and make a sort of calzone-type meal. Bake until bread dough is cooked through and the sauce is hot. You'll have a pizza that any reputable pizzeria would envy. It's quick, easy, and extremely satisfying.

An important part of the backpacking experience is great food. I believe that the weight of the food is less important than the quality and the taste. I also feel that spending a little time cooking is a small sacrifice for a great meal!

JEFFREY HARE
CITRUS HEIGHTS, CALIFORNIA

Piute Mountain Pizza

Total weight: 6 ounces
Total servings: 1

1 (5-ounce) bag Boboli
   Pizza Sauce

2 pitas

1 ounce cheddar cheese

1 tablespoon oil

$\frac{1}{3}$ cup water

Other toppings (optional)

At home:
Dehydrate Boboli Pizza Sauce on plastic wrap in a food dehydrator. Boboli is a bit tart, so add a little sugar before dehydrating if you like a sweeter sauce. When it dries to the consistency of tough leather, rip into pieces and place in a sandwich-size resealable plastic bag. Pack pitas, cheese, and oil separately.

On the trail:
Add water (more if needed) to Boboli mix in a resealable plastic bag. Knead the bag to help rehydrate the sauce. This will take a few minutes. Cut cheese into small pieces. Heat oil in frying pan. Cut a 3-inch slice into the side of each whole pita, enough to cause the inside to separate. Once the sauce sufficiently rehydrates, cut a small hole in the corner of the bag and shoot the sauce into the holes of each pita. Stuff your cheese into the pita along with anything else you'd like to add. Place in the hot frying pan over medium heat and cook both sides. You can cover the pan, but make sure the pitas don't burn. When cheese is melted, it's ready.

Authors' note
This recipe is amazingly delicious and curbs the universal pizza craving we all acquire during a long trip.

The Piute Mountains are considered a subrange of the Southern Sierra. They are a beautiful island of greenery rising up from the surrounding barren desert. It is an area difficult to access; and as a result, one can find solitude there away from the craziness of Southern California. The Pacific Crest Trail climbs up out of the heat of the Mojave Desert and over this island paradise before dropping once again into the arid valley of Kelso. If it was not for the Pacific Crest Trail, enjoying the area would be a somewhat risky business, as much of the land is privately held. We have spent a lot of time hiking the Pacific Crest Trail through the Piute Mountains, and it is high on our list of favorite places.

TIM AND CHRISTINE CONNERS
CINCINNATI, OHIO

Nutritional information per serving

calories	630
protein	19 g
carbohydrates	76 g
sodium	1,480 mg
fiber	3 g
fat	28 g
cholesterol	35 mg

Kirk's No-Cook Pizza

1 (5-ounce) bag Boboli
   Pizza Sauce

2 tablespoons Parmesan
   cheese

2 pitas

⅓ cup water

Total weight: 6 ounces
Total servings: 1

At home:
Dehydrate Boboli Pizza Sauce on dehydrator tray lined with plastic wrap. When it dries to the consistency of tough leather, tear into pieces and place in a sandwich-size resealable plastic bag along with Parmesan cheese. Store pitas separately in breathable wrap.

On the trail:
Add water (more if needed) to the resealable plastic bag containing the Boboli. Knead until sauce rehydrates. This will take a few minutes. Spread sauce over the tops of both pitas and eat. No cooking is required.

KIRK IKENS
ROGERS CITY, MICHIGAN

Nutritional information per serving

calories	460
protein	20 g
carbohydrates	76 g
sodium	150 mg
fiber	3 g
fat	9 g
cholesterol	15 mg

Brower's Baco Spuds

Total weight: 12 ounces
Weight per serving: 6 ounces
Total servings: 2

At home:

In a food dehydrator, dry chicken and vegetables. Place dried chicken and vegetables in a plastic bag and label it. Place the remaining ingredients, except gravy, in another bag. Keep gravy in its original package.

On the trail:

About 1 hour before cooking, rehydrate dried chicken and vegetables in bag with a small amount of water. Place 3 cups of water in a pot with only the veggie-meat ingredients and bring to a boil. Add the ingredients in the second bag and stir. Add extra water as needed. Mix gravy according to the directions on the package, and pour over the potatoes when they're done.

This is a basic recipe that I've been using for years. It's filling and has just the right amount of salt to quench that craving.

Ursula Brower
South Lake Tahoe, California

1 (5-ounce) can of chicken

4 ounces frozen mixed vegetables

$1\frac{1}{2}$ cups potato flakes

$\frac{1}{3}$ cup powdered milk

1 individual package Butter Buds

1 teaspoon dried parsley

1 teaspoon dried onion (or chives)

$\frac{1}{2}$ teaspoon pepper

$\frac{1}{2}$ cup Bacos

1 package gravy mix (your choice)

3 cups water, plus more as needed

Nutritional information per serving

calories	560
protein	39 g
carbohydrates	78 g
sodium	1,740 mg
fiber	4 g
fat	12 g
cholesterol	55 mg

Irwin's Forester Pass Mashed Potatoes

1 pound frozen mixed vegetables

$\frac{1}{4}$ cup Bob's Red Mill TVP (textured vegetable protein)

1 package Knorr Instant Gravy

1 cup powdered mashed potatoes

$3\frac{1}{2}$ cups water, plus more as needed

Total weight: 7 ounces
Weight per serving: 3.5 ounces
Total servings: 2

At home:
Chop up vegetables, then dry in a food dehydrator. Place TVP and vegetables together in a 1-gallon resealable plastic bag. Carry gravy and mashed potatoes separately.

On the trail:
Place the water in a pot. Rehydrate vegetables and TVP in water for about 1 hour. Bring water to a boil and add gravy. Stir continuously. Check vegetables occasionally and add additional water as needed to rehydrate. Add powdered mashed potatoes to mixture and stir.

IRWIN REEVES
BEAUMONT, CALIFORNIA

Most of my hiking is in the Sierra where it gets cold when the sun goes down. I always add a little extra water when cooking dinner and use it to make myself a cup of instant soup while the main course is cooking. It serves as an appetizer while warming me right up!

URSULA BROWER
SOUTH LAKE TAHOE, CALIFORNIA

Nutritional information per serving

calories	340
protein	21 g
carbohydrates	63 g
sodium	1,250 mg
fiber	9 g
fat	5 g
cholesterol	10 mg

Thru-Hiker Veggie Spaghetti

Total weight: 1 pound 3 ounces
Weight per serving: 6.3 ounces
Total servings: 3

At home:

Simmer spaghetti sauce in a pan. Chop the frozen vegetables into smaller pieces and sauté them with bell pepper and onion in olive oil just to soften.

Add vegetables to the spaghetti sauce and cook until vegetables are tender. Let cool. Purée spaghetti sauce-vegetable mix in a food processor until there are no lumps. Ladle 1¼-cup portions of sauce onto each of three drying trays covered with plastic wrap. Dry sauce in a food dehydrator until it has the consistency of leather (17 to 21 hours). Package each serving in a 1-gallon resealable plastic bag. Add ¼ cup of Parmesan cheese and ¼ teaspoon of salt to each serving bag.

Divide dried pasta into three separate servings of 4 ounces each. Store each in a 1-gallon resealable plastic bag. Carry each portion of pasta separately.

On the trail:

Begin rehydrating the spaghetti leather 1 hour before you plan to eat dinner, while you're still on the trail. Place one serving of leather and 1¼ cups water in a sealable plastic container. The leather will rehydrate faster if you rip it into pieces. Carefully place container back in your pack while you walk your last hour. Seal the container inside a plastic bag to be sure it won't leak into your pack. When you reach camp, the sloshing around in the backpack will have produced a wonderful fresh-tasting sauce with all of the vegetables you'll be craving.

(continued on next page)

Spaghetti leather:

1 (26-ounce) can vegetarian spaghetti sauce

1 (16-ounce) bag of frozen blended vegetables

½ tablespoon olive oil (more may be needed if using fresh vegetables)

¼ cup chopped bell peppers

¼ cup dried onion flakes

¾ cup Parmesan cheese

¾ teaspoon salt

3¾ cups water (1¼ cup per serving) to rehydrate spaghetti leather

Pasta:

4 ounces angel-hair pasta per serving of spaghetti leather

1¾ cups water per serving to boil pasta (use more as required)

Nutritional information per serving

calories	710
protein	30 g
carbohydrates	116 g
sodium	2,190 mg
fiber	7 g
fat	14 g
cholesterol	16 mg

(Thru-Hiker Veggie Spaghetti continued)

When you are ready to eat, bring 1¾ cups of water to a boil. Break in half one serving of the pasta and add to water, stirring for 2 to 3 minutes or until al dente. Drain any remaining water. With experience, you will be able to adjust the water amount so that there is none left over by the time the pasta is finished cooking—the noodles will have absorbed it completely.

Next, you have two options: Either dump the hot pasta into the rehydrated sauce in your plastic container and eat it lukewarm, which will be fine on a hot day; or dump the sauce into the pot of pasta and heat it all the way through, which makes for a little more cleanup.

I ate this meal two out of every three nights on my 1996 thru-hike on the Pacific Crest Trail and always looked forward to it. The spaghetti gives a great energy boost and is delicious!

DIANE KING
SOMERS, CONNECTICUT

Ballou's Turkey Spaghetti

Total weight: 1 pound 2 ounces
Weight per serving: 4.5 ounces
Total servings: 4

1 yellow onion, diced

½ teaspoon canola oil

1 pound ground turkey

½ teaspoon garlic salt

1 teaspoon dried oregano

1 (1¾-pound) jar Ragu Chunky Garden Style Spaghetti Sauce

8 ounces spaghetti

At home:

Sauté the diced onion in oil until translucent. Add ground turkey, garlic salt, and oregano, and sauté until cooked. Drain off any fat. Add spaghetti sauce. Stir and remove from heat.

In a separate pan, add pasta to 2 quarts boiling water and allow to cook until tender, stirring periodically. When cooked, drain spaghetti and add sauce mixture. Divide spaghetti evenly on 2 lightly oiled cookie sheets (15½x10¼x¾-inch). Spread spaghetti mix evenly over the cookie sheets. To dry the mixture, place cookie sheets on racks in the middle of an oven at the lowest temperature setting. When the spaghetti is brittle through and through, remove cookie sheets from the oven and cool. (You may also dry the mixture in a food dehydrator, spreading the spaghetti over plastic wrap-covered trays. While drying, break the spaghetti apart with your hands every 2 hours.) Divide each sheet of spaghetti evenly into two separate 1-gallon resealable plastic bags (four bags total). Store in refrigerator until ready to leave on your trip. If dried properly, each bag should keep for approximately six months.

On the trail:

Add enough water to barely cover the spaghetti in a pot and bring to a boil. The spaghetti will cook much more quickly than if it had not been precooked. Some presoaking may be desirable at very high elevations.

BOB BALLOU
SACRAMENTO, CALIFORNIA

Nutritional information per serving

calories	540
protein	31 g
carbohydrates	73 g
sodium	1,060 mg
fiber	7 g
fat	16 g
cholesterol	90 mg

Speedy Spaghetti

5 ounces sliced green beans

3 ounces sliced olives

8 ounces diced onions

8 ounces diced fresh mushrooms

6 ounces spaghetti

1 (28-ounce) bottle Prego Garden Spaghetti Sauce (or your choice)

½ pound ground sirloin

4 cups water

Total weight: 17 ounces
Weight per serving: 8.5 ounces
Total servings: 2

At home:

Dry all vegetables in your food dehydrator. Boil spaghetti noodles until tender, then dehydrate them. Dry the spaghetti sauce on plastic wrap in the dehydrator until it has the consistency of fruit leather. When finished, turn the sauce to powder in a food processor or rip it by hand into small pieces.

Fry sirloin until thoroughly cooked. Use paper towels to absorb the fat and then rinse with hot water in a colander to further remove the oils. Thoroughly dry the meat in the dehydrator until it is hard. Place spaghetti leather, dried vegetables, and dried meat in a resealable plastic bag. Place spaghetti noodles in a separate bag.

On the trail:

Add the water to the dehydrated sauce bag at least 1 hour before you are ready to cook. Mix from time to time. Add more water if needed. While waiting for the sauce to rehydrate, boil the noodles in 2 quarts of water and drain. Set aside. With the sauce rehydrated, place it in a separate pot. Heat the mix and add additional water as required. Add noodles and serve.

PAM COZ-HILL
VISALIA, CALIFORNIA

Author's Note:
Cooking the noodles before the trip helps speed up the cooking process on the trail.

Nutritional information per serving

calories	1,020
protein	49 g
carbohydrates	131 g
sodium	1,820 mg
fiber	13 g
fat	30 g
cholesterol	94 mg

Gard's Glacier Spaghetti

Total weight: 10 ounces
Total servings: 1

At home:
Package Parmesan cheese, garlic powder, onion powder, Bacos, salt, and pepper together in a resealable plastic bag. Carry oil and pasta separately.

On the trail:
Cook spaghetti in water until done, then drain. Stir in olive oil, then add Parmesan mixture. Mix thoroughly.

DAN GARD
MISSOULA, MONTANA

$\frac{1}{2}$ cup Parmesan cheese

2 teaspoons garlic powder

1 teaspoon onion powder

2 tablespoons Bacos

$\frac{1}{8}$ teaspoon salt

$\frac{1}{4}$ teaspoon pepper

6 ounces spaghetti

2 quarts water

1 tablespoon olive oil

Nutritional information per serving

calories	1,100
protein	50 g
carbohydrates	146 g
sodium	1,030 mg
fiber	1 g
fat	34 g
cholesterol	32 mg

Smitty's Favorite Spaghetti

15 large Roma tomatoes

8 ounces angel-hair pasta

2 garlic cloves

½ cup TVP (textured vegetable protein)

1 (1½-ounce) package dried spaghetti seasoning mix

1 quart water

Total weight: 14 ounces
Weight per serving: 7 ounces
Total servings: 2

At home:
Cut Roma tomatoes ¼-inch thick and dry in a food dehydrator. Place tomatoes, pasta, garlic cloves, and TVP into a 1-gallon resealable plastic bag. Keep spaghetti seasoning mix in its own pouch.

On the trail:
Chop garlic well. Bring the water to a boil and drop in the spaghetti-pasta mix. The tomatoes and TVP will reconstitute in 5 to 10 minutes, depending upon altitude. When the noodles are soft, add the seasoning mix and stir until all the powder is dissolved. Divide and eat.

Feast option: Serve with hard rolls, split and toasted. Dessert can be a few cookies and hot coffee with honey and cinnamon.

This is my favorite meal and I fix it every time that I go out.

CRAIG SMITH
"SMITTY"
SPRINGFIELD, MISSOURI

Nutritional information per serving

calories	670
protein	32 g
carbohydrates	127 g
sodium	1,490 mg
fiber	11 g
fat	4 g
cholesterol	0 mg

White Trash Pasta

Total weight: 8 ounces
Total servings: 1

At home:
Chop the broccoli into fine pieces. Dry in a food dehydrator. Mix all ingredients (except water) together and place in a resealable plastic bag.

On the trail:
Pour all ingredients into water in a pot and bring to a boil. Allow to simmer 5 to 10 minutes until the broccoli is rehydrated.

This recipe works great if you are resupplying in a town and need dinners that don't require too much thought or money. For some reason, I never got tired of eating White Trash Pasta. Maybe it was because I was raised on casseroles from *Good Housekeeping* magazine.

CRAIG GIFFEN
PORTLAND, OREGON

As I travel along the trail, I sometimes realize that the food I have remaining in my pack may not last until the next town. So I build a gleaner's bag using a resealable plastic bag. Depending on how short the food supply will be, I donate one to two spoonfuls per meal to my gleaner's bag. After I run out of my planned meals, I divide the contents of the gleaner's bag by the number of trail days left to town.

WILL O'DAIX
"THE GREEN GHOST"
INDIANAPOLIS, INDIANA

1 (16-ounce) bag frozen broccoli

1 (4½-ounce) package Lipton Cheddar and Broccoli Rice and Sauce

½ cup Minute Instant Brown Rice

2½ cups water

Nutritional information per serving

calories	850
protein	33 g
carbohydrates	150 g
sodium	2,100 mg
fiber	4 g
fat	22 g
cholesterol	45 mg

Outdoor Pesto Tortellini

4 ounces Roma tomatoes

4 ounces fresh
mushrooms

1½ ounces (¼ of a 6-ounce
can) of olives

1 bell pepper

1 (½-ounce) package
Schilling Pesto Sauce
Mix

2 teaspoons garlic powder

2 tablespoons Parmesan
cheese

¼ cup olive oil

1 (8-ounce) package of
dried tortellini

½ cup water

Dried pepperoni chunks,
pine nuts, or jerky
chunks (optional)

Total weight: 12 ounces
Weight per serving: 6 ounces
Total servings: 2

At home:

Slice and dry the tomatoes, mushrooms, olives, and
bell pepper in a food dehydrator. Place dried vegetables in a 1-gallon resealable plastic bag and add
pesto sauce, garlic powder, and Parmesan cheese.
Carry oil and pasta separately.

On the trail:

Add the water to vegetable-pesto sauce mix and
knead in bag. Reseal bag so mixture doesn't dry out,
and allow it to sit for 30 minutes. Add more water if
needed. After allowing the vegetables to rehydrate,
begin to boil 2.5 quarts of water for the tortellini.
Add the tortellini and boil until rehydrated and hot,
then drain. Add vegetable-pesto sauce mix and oil to
tortellini and stir over low heat (adding more water
as needed).

Jeffrey Hare
Citrus Heights, California

Nutritional
information
per serving

calories	830
protein	26 g
carbohydrates	78 g
sodium	2,270 mg
fiber	4 g
fat	43 g
cholesterol	88 mg

Michigan Salmon Fettuccine

Total weight: 14 ounces
Weight per serving: 7 ounces
Total servings: 2

2 (6-ounce) cans of
salmon

2 packs (4.4 ounces each)
Lipton Alfredo
Noodles and Sauce

1 packet Butter Buds

$\frac{1}{3}$ cup powdered milk

3 cups water

At home:

Dry salmon thoroughly in the dehydrator and place in a sandwich-size resealable plastic bag. In a separate resealable plastic bag, combine the dry noodles and sauce, Butter Buds, and powdered milk.

On the trail:

Place water in pan with salmon and allow to sit for 20 minutes. Bring to a boil and add the rest of the ingredients. Reduce heat and allow noodles to rehydrate for 5 minutes or more. Add more water if needed.

JOAN YOUNG
SCOTTVILLE, MICHIGAN

Nutritional information per serving

calories	770
protein	58 g
carbohydrates	91 g
sodium	3,050 mg
fiber	4 g
fat	22 g
cholesterol	285 mg

Tahoe Chicken Curry

3 (5-ounce) cans light chunk chicken

8 ounces frozen peas

1½ cups instant brown rice

1½ teaspoons curry powder

¼ teaspoon pepper (or to taste)

½ cup unsalted halved cashews

½ cup raisins

2 chicken bouillon cubes

2 cups water

Total weight: 1 pound 1 ounce
Weight per serving: 8.5 ounces
Total servings: 2

At home:
Dry chicken and peas in a food dehydrator. In a bowl, mix together the dried chicken and peas and add the rest of the ingredients, except the bouillon cubes and water. Package the mix for the trail.

On the trail:
Bring water to a boil. Add both bouillon cubes. Add dried dinner mix. Allow to cook about 1 minute. Remove from heat and let sit 5 minutes, or until the rice is tender.

URSULA BROWER
SOUTH LAKE TAHOE, CALIFORNIA

Weigh everything. If you think it's all too heavy, substitute something lighter. I would not recommend carrying a sixty-five pound pack, but bringing a little extra food and fuel is not a bad thing.

JEFFREY HARE
CITRUS HEIGHTS, CALIFORNIA

Nutritional information per serving

calories	770
protein	40 g
carbohydrates	119 g
sodium	1,290 mg
fiber	8 g
fat	22 g
cholesterol	75 mg

Cascade Valley Chicken and Rice

Total weight: 9 ounces
Weight per serving: 4.5 ounces
Total servings: 2

At home:
In a food dehydrator, dehydrate chicken and peas. In a 1-gallon resealable plastic bag, mix together chicken, peas, and bouillon cubes. Store rice separately.

On the trail:
Add dehydrated chicken, peas, and bouillon to water in a pot. Bring water to a boil. Add instant rice and stir well. Remove from heat. Cover and let stand 10 minutes. A pat of butter improves flavor but is not necessary.

This meal is a quick and easy staple for any of our backpack trips, long or short. We can make this in the dark, in the snow, in the wind, and in the rain. And cleanup is easy because it has no oil or sauce. This was another of our rotating Pacific Crest Trail dinners. I still like this one and use it today for nearly every backpacking trip.

ANN MARSHALL
PORT ORCHARD, WASHINGTON

1 (5-ounce) can of light chunk chicken

4 ounces frozen peas

2 chicken bouillon cubes

2 cups instant brown rice

1 tablespoon butter (optional)

$2\frac{1}{2}$ cups water

Nutritional information per serving:
(without butter)

calories	450
protein	15 g
carbohydrates	92 g
sodium	1,110 mg
fiber	6 g
fat	4 g
cholesterol	8 mg

You-Don't-Need-Drawings-to-Do-It Poached Trout

¼ teaspoon dried basil

¼ teaspoon dried rosemary

¼ teaspoon dried thyme

¼ teaspoon dried ground sage

¼ teaspoon salt

¼ teaspoon pepper

Any herb or spice that pleases your palate (optional)

1 vegetable bouillon cube

2 fresh-caught, medium-size trout, gutted, well cleaned, with skin on

Water

Weight of spices: less than 1 ounce
Total servings: 2

At home:
Mix the herbs together in a bag.

On the trail:
Add seasoning mix and 1 bouillon cube to a pan of water (ideally about the size of a large coffee can). Bring the water nearly to a boil so that the bouillon cube is dissolved and the liquid is an aromatic weak herb broth. Add trout and cover with water. (You may have to cut larger fish in half to fit into most backpack cook pots.) When water returns to near boiling, cover pan and allow fish to simmer on low heat for 2 minutes. Remove from heat and poach for 10 minutes until flesh is firm (white or light pink, depending on the species) and cooked through to the backbone. Trout is done when the filets on each side can be stripped off the bones easily. Strip off and discard the fins and their short bones. The skin is good to eat, but some folks prefer not to eat it.

Trout are easy to catch in the wilderness and a great natural protein and fat food source. But I seldom have the oil or grease and spiced flour to fry them up golden crispy once I leave the trailhead. Whenever I try to cook trout over the open campfire, I usually end up scorching the skin, drying out the flesh, or undercooking the meat near the bones. Poached trout is a delicious, lightweight alternative.

In 1976–79, I lived in Orofino, Idaho, about 50 miles downriver from the Selway-Bitterroot Wilderness. My favorite holiday hangouts were Stanley Hot Springs on Boulder Creek and Jerry Johnson Hot Springs on Warm Springs Creek. One summer holiday week, we shared a wilderness campsite near the springs with a couple of young free spirits who parked an old hippie yellow school

Nutritional information per serving

calories	380
protein	65 g
carbohydrates	0 g
sodium	100 mg
fiber	0 g
fat	11 g
cholesterol	188 mg

bus (their home) just off the highway at the Warm Springs Trailhead footbridge. The young man fished every day, and they lived off the land as much as possible. (That was the "good old days" before these sites became "happening" places in nude bathing guides and before the Forest Service shut down all overnight camping within ¼ mile of most hot springs.) The lady of the camp prepared the most delicious poached trout.

ROY TRYON
CALIFORNIA CITY, CALIFORNIA

Authors' note

Roy is an architect and a friend of ours from the days when we worked at NASA. In addition to sending us this great recipe idea, Roy promised that he would also send us drawings showing how to clean a trout. We were happy to hear this and even went so far as to purchase a fresh trout from the grocery store for him to use as a model. Well, weeks turned into months, months turned into years, and we still hadn't received any drawings. First we asked nicely, then we begged, and finally we badgered. Roy, in his sweet manner, would reply, "Oh yeah, gotta getcha those drawings." Still we received nothing. Eventually, we gave up but not before one final dig at the master procrastinator. This recipe was originally called Poached Trout. We decided to rename it. As you will see, we also took the liberty of renaming Roy's bread-on-a-stick recipe. We hope it encourages him to mend his ways!

Tamale Pie for Ungrateful Waifs

½ teaspoon pepper

½ teaspoon dried sage

¼ teaspoon dried thyme

¼ teaspoon ground allspice

¼ teaspoon paprika

1 pound low-fat ground sirloin

1 (14-ounce) can whole pitted olives (6 ounces drained), halved

1 (5¼-ounce) can kidney beans

1 (8-ounce) can diced chilies, packed in water

¼ cup chopped dried tomatoes

1 cup masa harina (corn flour)

1 tablespoon chili powder

¼ teaspoon ground cumin

1 packet Lipton Instant Onion Soup Mix

2 cups water to rehydrate one serving from Bag A

⅓ cup of water added to one serving from Bag B

Nutritional information per serving

calories	880
protein	52 g
carbohydrates	73 g
sodium	1,980 mg
fiber	14 g
fat	44 g
cholesterol	138 mg

Total weight: 14 ounces
Weight per serving: 4.7 ounces
Total servings: 3

At home:

Add pepper, sage, thyme, allspice, and paprika to ground sirloin. Brown mixture in a skillet. When cooked, remove excess fat by spreading the meat over a paper towel. Place a second paper towel over the sirloin. Place a cutting board over the paper towel and press the fat out onto the towels. (It is very important to remove fat from the meat prior to drying since fat can become rancid.)

Spread the ground sirloin onto plastic wrap placed on drying trays and dry in dehydrator until it has the consistency of bacon bits. Place olives, kidney beans, and diced chilies one layer deep on dehydrator trays and dry. Then place everything from your dehydrator (dried ground sirloin, olives, kidney beans, and chilies) and the tomatoes into a bowl. Divide sirloin mixture into three separate servings by placing 1 cup of the mixture into each of three separate resealable plastic bags each. Label each of these bags "Tamale Pie A."

In a separate bowl, mix together masa harina, chili powder, cumin, and contents of onion soup packet. Divide this into three separate servings by placing ⅓ cup of mixture into each of three sandwich-size resealable plastic bags. Label each of these bags "Tamale Pie B."

On the trail:

To make one serving while setting up camp, place one serving of Bag A and 2 cups of water in your pot and allow ingredients to rehydrate. Check periodically to see if you need to add more water to keep the ingredients rehydrating properly. When the contents of Bag A are rehydrated, add the contents of Bag B and another ⅓ cup water. Heat slowly over a low flame, stirring continuously until thick. Shut off flame and cover. Let set for about 5 minutes. The pie will have the consistency of porridge.

This is another unique addition to our backpacking dinner fare. We love the flavor of Mexican food and had been missing it on the trail. I was inspired by traditional ingredients for this recipe.

Our "food group" has also referred to my tamale pie as "tamale mush" or "tamale gruel" because the texture is straight out of Oliver Twist's orphanage kitchen. While commenting on the tamale pie, they nonetheless gobble it up and ask for seconds. Those ungrateful waifs!

PAM COZ-HILL
VISALIA, CALIFORNIA

Katahdin Tamale Pie

1 medium green pepper, chopped

1 cup frozen corn

1 package Knorr Tomato and Basil Soup Mix

¼ cup TVP (textured vegetable protein)

3 tablespoons dried onion

1 (1-ounce) package Lawry's Taco Seasoning

1 teaspoon chili powder

¼ teaspoon crushed dried red pepper

½ teaspoon instant minced garlic

¼ teaspoon dried oregano

¼ teaspoon ground cumin

1 teaspoon paprika

½ teaspoon cornstarch

1 (8½-ounce) package Jiffy Corn Muffin Mix

⅓ cup water for corn muffin mix

3 cups water for soup mix

Total weight: 1 pound
Weight per serving: 8 ounces
Total servings: 2

At home:

Dry green pepper and corn in a food dehydrator. Blend together all dry ingredients except Jiffy mix and water. Store in sandwich-size resealable plastic bag. Pour corn muffin mix into separate sandwich-size resealable plastic bag.

On the trail:

Pour tamale sauce mixture into pan along with 3 cups of water. Bring to a boil and allow to cook for about 3 minutes. Add ⅓ cup water to the bag of cornmeal mix, and mush around until it becomes a dough. Cut a small hole at one of the corners of your dough bag and squeeze the dough out evenly onto the top of the tamale sauce. Reduce the heat to very low, cover the pan, and steam for about 10 minutes. The recipe is ready when an inserted toothpick (or stick or knife blade) comes out clean. Be careful not to let the mixture burn.

WALT AND JANE DANIELS
MOHEGAN LAKE, NEW YORK

Author's note:

To reduce sodium content, use low-sodium TVP, which is usually available at health-food stores.

Nutritional information per serving

calories	820
protein	19 g
carbohydrates	140 g
sodium	3,290 mg
fiber	9 g
fat	21 g
cholesterol	0 mg

Sandy's Weed Salad

At home:
Store dressing in a plastic squeeze bottle.

On the trail:
Collect greens along the way in a plastic sack and wash them in streams. Cut them fine and place in a 1-quart plastic bag. Toss in 2 tablespoons of dressing. This salad is a refreshing treat for a long-distance hiker.

Eating greens along the way is a great provider of calcium. The dandelion, plantain, chicory and chick weed, yellow dock, lamb's quarter, sheep sorrel, and miner's lettuce are abundant in the Sierra at elevations between 3,000 and 6,000 feet between July and early August.

Pick fresh weeds and herbal greens gathered from the sides of the trail if they look clean and fresh.

SANDY LEE BURNS
PROSPECT, OREGON

Authors' note
You must know how to positively identify plants before using Sandy's recipe. If unsure, don't pick! Also, smell the greens before picking to ensure that they are fresh and not contaminated. Wash them thoroughly after picking.

Miner's lettuce

Dandelion

Plantain

Yellow dock

Sheep sorrel

Lamb's quarter

Red clover

Chicory and chick weed

Wild and prickly lettuce

Bull thistle (if you can get past the prickles)

Dressing:
Fresh squeezed lemon, mineral seasoning, and olive oil (or dressing of your choice).

Nutritional information per serving
Dependent upon the types of greens and dressing you use.

Night-after-Night No-Cook Bean Soup

5 pounds bean and barley mix

10 ounces frozen mixed vegetables

6 pounds Roma tomatoes

6 pounds onions

2 tablespoons Vege-Sal

1 teaspoon garlic powder

10 ramen seasoning packets (no noodles)

3 cups of water per serving

Total weight: 6 pounds 3 ounces
Weight per serving: 5 ounces
Total servings: 20

At home:

To prepare the bean and barley mix, allow it to soak overnight in a large pot. In the morning, drain off water. Add fresh water, then boil until soft. Drain and rinse the cooked mix. Spread on dehydrator trays and dry.

To make the spice-vegetable mix, thinly slice mixed vegetables, tomatoes, and onions, and place in a dehydrator to dry. After drying, blend in a food processor or blender until very fine. Combine this vegetable mix with the Vege-Sal, garlic powder, and ramen seasonings. In each of twenty separate sandwich-size resealable plastic bags, combine 1 cup of beans with 4 tablespoons of spice-vegetable mix.

On the trail:

For each serving, add 3 cups of water to the mix in a pot and allow it to stand 1 hour if using hot water, 2 hours if cold water. May be eaten hot or cold.

We ate this every night on a 35-day Pacific Crest Trail hike and never got tired of it. We even eat it at home.

Marion Davison
Apple Valley, California

Nutritional information per serving

calories	340
protein	28 g
carbohydrates	90 g
sodium	1,320 mg
fiber	42 g
fat	1 g
cholesterol	0 mg

Japanese Energy Soup

Total weight: 5 ounces
Total servings: 1

At home:
Dry tuna in a dehydrator. Mix dried tuna together with miso soup powder, rice, and sushi nori torn into small pieces.

On the trail:
Bring water to a boil. Add rice-tuna mix and stir frequently until rice is soft and tuna is rehydrated. Add more water if needed. This dish is super lightweight and nutritious!

JULIA VOGEL
PASADENA, CALIFORNIA

1 (6-ounce) can water-packed white tuna

1 (0.35-ounce) package of Westbrae Mellow White Miso Soup

1 cup Minute Rice

2 sheets of sushi nori (dried seaweed)

$2\frac{1}{2}$ cups water

Oriental food stores have a wide variety of dried foods. I've bought dried clams, which reconstitute very nicely. I've even tried dried seaweed.

RICK BOMBACI
ENTERPRISE, OREGON

Nutritional information per serving

calories	650
protein	45 g
carbohydrates	74 g
sodium	140 mg
fiber	6 g
fat	17 g
cholesterol	63 mg

Packer's Pea Soup

9 cups water

1 pound dried green split peas

1½ cups finely chopped carrots

1½ cups peeled and finely chopped sweet potatoes (or yams)

1 cup chopped onion

1 cup chopped celery

4 garlic cloves, minced (more if you like)

4 tablespoons oil

1 teaspoon ground marjoram

2 teaspoons dried basil (or half as much if fresh)

1 teaspoon ground cumin

3 bouillon cubes

Salt to taste (optional)

¼ cup brewer's yeast

2 cups water per serving

Total weight: 1 pound
Weight per serving: 4 ounces
Total servings: 4

At home:

In a large pot, bring water and peas to a boil; lower heat and simmer for 1 hour. Skim off and discard foam. In a separate pot, sauté carrots, potatoes, onion, celery, and garlic in oil for 10 minutes. Add seasonings to the sauté pan and cook for a few more minutes. Add sauté to the peas, along with brewer's yeast. Simmer for an additional hour, then test to see if it's ready. Add salt to taste. When the peas and vegetables are tender and the soup is thick, remove from heat and allow to cool, then place in a blender.

Blend until smooth and free of lumps. Cover four food dehydrator trays with plastic wrap and spoon 1¾ cups of the soup onto each tray, spreading it to within an inch of the edge. If your soup is too thin, it will be runny; if this is the case, put it back on the stove and heat until thick enough to stay put. Each tray will produce one serving.

When soup is quite dry and crackled, separately grind each tray's contents into a fine powder. A regular coffee grinder works great (just make sure you wipe all the residual coffee grounds out first). You can also crush the soup, using a rolling pin, between two sheets of wax paper. If you don't mind cooking the soup longer prior to drying, it will be thicker and once it's dehydrated you'll be able to break it into pieces with your hands. Package each tray of powder in a 1-quart resealable plastic bag.

On the trail:

For each serving, bring 2 cups of water to a boil and add one serving of soup. Stir well.

Ann Marshall
Port Orchard, Washington

Nutritional information per serving

calories	680
protein	33 g
carbohydrates	107 g
sodium	850 mg
fiber	23 g
fat	16 g
cholesterol	0 mg

Dog Food Soup

Total weight: 7 ounces
Weight per serving: 3.5 ounces
Total servings: 2

At home:
Dry peas and carrots in a food dehydrator. Mix together all dried and dry ingredients, breaking apart the ramen. Store in a resealable plastic bag.

On the trail:
Add all ingredients to water and simmer until vegetables are rehydrated and noodles are cooked. Reduce the cooking time by taking the pot off the flame and letting it sit for 5 minutes before eating. Stir occasionally while cooking. If mixture gets too thick, add a little more water.

During our meal planning for the Pacific Crest Trail, my hiking partner Lee and I tried to include meals we both liked. Generally we were successful, but this wasn't one of the successes. On our 1,000-mile trip through Oregon and Washington, Dog Food Soup was one of our four rotating dinners. I wasn't familiar with this dinner; it was one of his recipes. I tired of it quickly, and the TVP looked just like dog food kibbles. I named it Dog Food Soup. Lee still likes it.

Ann Marshall
Port Orchard, Washington

4 ounces frozen peas

8 ounces frozen carrots

1 envelope Lipton Beefy Onion Soup Mix

1 package ramen (including seasoning package)

$\frac{1}{2}$ cup TVP (textured vegetable protein)

1 quart water

Nutritional information per serving

calories	420
protein	23 g
carbohydrates	50 g
sodium	1,790 mg
fiber	9 g
fat	10 g
cholesterol	0 mg

Tree Frog Soup with Rattlesnake

4 serving-size cups Near East Dried Split Pea Soup

1 (12-ounce) tin of Spam

4 cups water

Total weight (includes Spam tin): 1 pound 5 ounces
Weight per serving: 10.5 ounces
Total servings: 2

Method 1:

At home:
Pour the contents of all four soup cups into a resealable plastic bag. Leave the cups at home. Carry Spam separately.

On the trail:
Chop Spam into small pieces. Heat water in pan. Add soup mix and Spam to pan and eat when soup is hot.

Method 2:

At home:
Pour the contents of all four soup cups into a resealable plastic bag. Telescope the soup cups (place one inside the other) and bring them along on the trail. Carry Spam separately.

On the trail:
Divide the dried soup among the four cups. Cut Spam into small pieces and divide evenly into the four cups. Heat the water and divide into each of the cups. Stir and eat when soup is rehydrated. (Saves pack volume and you don't have to clean the pot.)

Method 3:

At home:
Pour the contents of all four soup cups into a resealable plastic bag. Place the empty soup cups one inside the other and bring them along on the trail. Carry Spam separately.

Nutritional information per serving

calories	910
protein	47 g
carbohydrates	70 g
sodium	3,450 mg
fiber	16 g
fat	50 g
cholesterol	120 mg

On the trail:

Divide the soup among the four cups. Cut Spam into small pieces and divide evenly among the four cups. Pour about 8 ounces of water into each cup. Place cups in the sunlight and allow the solar rays to warm them. (Saves volume, messiness, and fuel!)

Trail purists note: I'm just kidding. The ingredients to my favorite trail meal are not really critters. I just call it that because it sounds cool, and it looks green and lumpy. I found this food to contain just what a thru-hiker's body needs: a lot of fat, salt, water, and green vegetable bulk. You also don't need a stove to prepare it (see method 3). Though it may sound too simple and too plain to be any good, Tree Frog Soup with Rattlesnake changed my life on the trail.

The first time I tried it, I was totally beat, totally beaten, ready to hitchhike back to so-called civilization and eat in a restaurant every night for the rest of my life. But Tree Frog Soup with Rattlesnake filled my belly and tickled my palate. In no time, I was virtually dancing with bears.

MARK DAVIS
"CRAWLS WITH BEARS"
SAN FRANCISCO, CALIFORNIA

Vermilion Valley Vegetable Soup

1 (16-ounce) package frozen corn kernels

1 (8-ounce) can sliced mushrooms

1 (16-ounce) bag frozen peas

1 package ramen noodles (any style)

2 packages Knorr Vegetable Soup Mix

½ cup dehydrated potato flakes

2 tablespoons dried onion flakes

1 teaspoon pepper

2 tablespoons garlic powder

2½ cups water per serving

Total weight: 1 pound 2 ounces
Weight per serving: 6 ounces
Total servings: 3

At home:
Dry the corn, mushrooms, and peas, and place in a large bowl. Break up ramen noodles into small pieces and add to bowl with vegetable soup mix. Blend all ingredients together. Place 1½ cups of the mixture per serving into each of three sandwich-size resealable plastic bags.

On the trail:
For each serving, add one bag of soup mix to 2½ cups of water. Bring to a boil and cook until vegetables are fully rehydrated.

A hiking buddy of mine named Scott Norton gave me this recipe.

JEFFREY HARE
CITRUS HEIGHTS, CALIFORNIA

Authors' note:
To reduce sodium content, omit ramen seasoning package.

Nutritional information per serving

calories	570
protein	25 g
carbohydrates	107 g
sodium	3,180 mg
fiber	15 g
fat	7 g
cholesterol	0 mg

Lassen Volcanic Eruption Chili

Total weight: 16 ounces
Weight per serving: 8 ounces
Total servings: 2

At home:

Place the beans in a colander and rinse. Dry the beans in a single layer in the dehydrator until they are crumbly. Cook the ground beef thoroughly in a skillet. Drain the fat well. Place the cooked meat in a colander and rinse thoroughly with hot water to remove as much fat as possible. Dry the meat in the dehydrator until it resembles coarse gravel; it must be hard and dry.

Dry the sliced tomatoes, cayenne or jalapeño peppers, and bell pepper in the dehydrator. The tomato slices will be hard and leathery when finished; the pepper will be brittle. Take all the dried ingredients (beans, meat, tomatoes, and peppers) and place in a resealable plastic bag along with the packet of chili seasoning. If you will not be using this meal soon, it will keep in a freezer for well over a year or sealed, in a cool, dark, and dry environment, for about one month. Regardless, ensure that the meat has not spoiled before using it.

On the trail:

The rehydrating can be performed in a plastic container or bag while you continue to hike to your dinner location, or you can rehydrate the mix in a pot when you arrive at your camp. To make two servings, add the water to chili contents and allow to rehydrate for about 1 hour. Add more water if needed. Once rehydrated, heat the mix in a pot along with the chili seasoning.

CRAIG SMITH
"SMITTY"
SPRINGFIELD, MISSOURI

2 (15-ounce) cans black beans (or your choice)

1 pound very lean ground beef

8 Roma tomatoes, sliced $\frac{1}{4}$-inch thick

3 cayenne or jalapeño peppers (more or fewer, to taste)

1 bell pepper, sliced in strips

1 (1.48-ounce) package Lawry's Chili Seasoning

1 quart water

Nutritional information per serving

calories	1,050
protein	39 g
carbohydrates	92 g
sodium	1,500 mg
fiber	20 g
fat	39 g
cholesterol	210 mg

Smoky Mountain Chili

1 (15-ounce) can kidney beans

1 (15-ounce) can pinto beans (or black beans)

8 ounces Pace Thick and Chunky Salsa

1 cup TVP (textured vegetable protein)

1 package chili seasoning mix

5 cups water

Total weight: 12 ounces
Weight per serving: 6 ounces
Total servings: 2

At home:
Rinse beans and dry them in your dehydrator. Pour salsa onto plastic wrap on a dehydrator tray and dry until it becomes leatherlike. Tear salsa leather into small pieces. Combine all the ingredients into a resealable plastic bag along with the package of seasoning mix.

On the trail:
In a pot, combine all ingredients with water. Cook, stirring often, for about 15 minutes or until beans are soft. When cooking, you may have to stir almost constantly while holding the pot above the flame in order to keep the chili from scorching. It gets quite thick, so keep adding water as necessary. Serve with tortilla chips, rice, or all by itself.

Adolph's Chili Seasoning is a good choice for the spice mix. It comes with an extra-hot flavoring packet for those who like their chili "on fire."

This recipe was developed by a man from Florida whom I met on a trek in the Smoky Mountains. He served as a guide to two others and bought and prepared all their food for the entire trip. The other two did the cleanup and carried the tortilla chips. I would like to give him credit for this recipe, but I don't remember his name.

I cooked this chili on a rainy night on Grandfather Mountain in North Carolina (rain and wind compliments of Hurricane Fran), and my partner and I went from cold, wet, shivering hikers to warm, well fed, and happy in a matter of minutes!

Nutritional information per serving

calories	632
protein	52 g
carbohydrates	113 g
sodium	2,760 mg
fiber	31 g
fat	2 g
cholesterol	0 mg

MARTHA MANZANO
FALLS CHURCH, VIRGINIA

Hotter-than-the-Mojave Chili

Total weight: 1 pound
Weight per serving: 4 ounces
Total servings: 4

At home:

In a pan, fry the ground beef until thoroughly cooked. Drain fat, rinse in a colander using hot water, and pat dry with paper towels. In a large pot, combine all ingredients, including ground beef if using, along with 1 cup of water. Simmer until tender.

On each of four separate trays (covered in plastic wrap), place 2 cups of chili and dehydrate. Each tray will produce one serving. If using ground beef, make sure it is thoroughly dried. Break each tray of chili leather into small pieces and package each in a 1-gallon resealable plastic bag.

On the trail:

Add one bag of chili to 1½ cups of water per serving and heat until chili mix is fully rehydrated.

BRIAN GULDBERG
BOZEMAN, MONTANA

I add corn pasta elbows to my store-bought, pre-made, dehydrated meals for even more energy. I do this by packaging 4 ounces of corn elbows with each of my dehydrated meals prior to the hike.

STEVE FUQUAY
"SWITCHBACK"
LAS VEGAS, NEVADA

1 pound lean ground beef (optional)

1 (28-ounce) can whole tomatoes

2 (6-ounce) cans tomato paste

1 rounded tablespoon chili powder

1½ teaspoons cumin seed

1 tablespoon ground mustard

1 tablespoon garlic powder

1½ teaspoons cayenne

1 tablespoon honey

2 tablespoons soy sauce

1 medium onion, finely chopped

1 medium green pepper, finely chopped

1 cup finely sliced mushrooms

1 (28-ounce) can chili beans

1 cup water

1½ cups of water to rehydrate

Nutritional information per serving

calories	660
protein	51 g
carbohydrates	67 g
sodium	1,960 mg
fiber	9 g
fat	19 g
cholesterol	105 mg

Campo Corn Chowder

5 Yukon Gold potatoes (or regular if Yukons are unavailable)

4 cups low-fat milk

1 large onion, chopped

2 cloves garlic, minced

1 tablespoon butter

$\frac{1}{2}$ teaspoon dried oregano

$\frac{1}{8}$ teaspoon dried sage

1 teaspoon salt

$\frac{1}{2}$ teaspoon ground pepper

$\frac{1}{2}$ teaspoon dried thyme

2 vegetable bouillon cubes

4 cups frozen or fresh corn

$\frac{1}{2}$ cup chopped bell pepper

$\frac{1}{2}$ cup minced scallions (or green onion)

2 cups water per serving

Total weight: 14 ounces
Weight per serving: 3.5 ounces
Total servings: 4

At home:

Boil potatoes in water, then drain, peel, and cube. Bring milk to a low boil in large pot and add potatoes, onion, garlic, butter, and all seasonings. Cover and simmer for 15 minutes, stirring occasionally. Add corn, bell pepper, and scallions. Cook until vegetables are tender. Blend mixture thoroughly in a blender. Pour 2¼ cups of soup onto each of four dehydrator trays covered in plastic wrap. Each tray will contain one serving. Dehydrate the soup into a brittle leather. For each serving, rip one tray's soup leather into small pieces and place in separate sandwich-size resealable plastic bags.

On the trail:

In a pot, add 2 cups of water to each serving of soup leather and let sit for 1 hour. Bring soup mix to a boil and cook until mix is fully rehydrated and smooth, stirring frequently. You can also bring the soup mix straight to a boil without the 1 hour of rehydrating, but you will use a little more fuel in doing so. Add more water if needed.

This recipe is named for the small town near the southern terminus of the Pacific Crest Trail. Driving home from a bike trip in Mexico several years ago, we stopped by the wood post monument erected at the border where the Pacific Crest Trail begins, just to take a look. It's a rather simple marker, but talk about the goosebumps knowing that that narrow dirt path winding down the hill and off to the north goes 2,638 miles all the way to Canada! We wanted to forget everything else and just start walking.

It's one thing to intellectualize it; it's another thing altogether to be there at the starting point and dream of walking that entire wilderness trail. If you are ever near the end point of a long-distance trail, stop by the terminal marker and check out the unexpected feelings you'll have. It will be worth the effort.

Nutritional information per serving

calories	500
protein	16 g
carbohydrates	91 g
sodium	1,220 mg
fiber	8 g
fat	8 g
cholesterol	27 mg

TIM AND CHRISTINE CONNERS
CINCINNATI, OHIO

Alaskan Chipped Beef Sauce

Total weight: 3.5 ounces
Weight per serving: 1.75 ounces
Total servings: 2

At home:
Dry beef even further in a food dehydrator and break into pieces. Mix beef, powdered milk, creamer, and flour together and store in a plastic bag. Store butter separately.

On the trail:
In a pan, melt the butter and mix with the dry ingredients and water. Heat and stir until thick.

This was one of our favorite meals to enjoy beneath the Harding Ice Flow and above Lake Tustamena in the Kenai Peninsula, Alaska. This sauce, when added to toast, instant rice, or mashed potatoes makes a delicious and easy meal.

JEFF AND CHRIS WALL
LANCASTER, CALIFORNIA

1 (4.5-ounce) jar Armour Sliced Dried Beef

$\frac{1}{3}$ cup Milkman low-fat powdered milk

1 tablespoon Coffee-mate non-dairy creamer

1 tablespoon flour

2 tablespoons butter

1 cup water

Nutritional information per serving:
(sauce only)

calories	290
protein	21 g
carbohydrates	14 g
sodium	2,890 mg
fiber	0 g
fat	15 g
cholesterol	86 mg

Backpackers' Potluck

1 (16-ounce) bag mixed frozen vegetables (lima beans, corn, carrots, peas, and green beans)

1 (5-ounce) can light chunk chicken

2 cups instant brown rice

1 package dried onion soup mix

$\frac{1}{8}$ teaspoon ground cayenne

1 tablespoon margarine

3 cups water (more if needed)

Courtesy The Daily Gazette *(Schenectady, NY)*

Total weight: 13 ounces
Weight per serving: 6.5 ounces
Total servings: 2

At home:
Dry vegetables and chicken separately in your dehydrator. Mix together dried vegetables, dried chicken, rice, onion soup, and cayenne. Place in a 1-gallon resealable plastic bag. Pack margarine separately.

On the trail:
Place all ingredients, including margarine, into water and allow to sit for about 30 minutes. Bring mixture to a boil and cook for 10 minutes. If the vegetables aren't sufficiently rehydrated, allow them to simmer a little longer.

This recipe was adapted from an article about backpacking food published in the Schenectady *Gazette* more than twenty years ago. The article described Backpackers' Potluck as a delicious trail dinner idea and an easy stew to prepare in the wild. We have served this meal in the wild multiple times to ourselves, our family, and youth groups over the past two decades. Here's how to prepare this simple, nutritious meal.

DAVID AND SANDRA GEISINGER
SCHENECTADY, NEW YORK

Nutritional information per serving

calories	700
protein	31 g
carbohydrates	122 g
sodium	1,590 mg
fiber	12 g
fat	11 g
cholesterol	43 mg

Trail-Grown Sprouts

Total weight: 1 ounce (not including netting)
Total servings: 4

$\frac{1}{8}$ **cup seeds (alfalfa, red clover, mung, or your choice)**

Water

Mosquito netting or gauze

On the trail:

Soak seeds in water for approximately 24 hours. Pour into mosquito netting. Place in an opaque plastic bag in your pack for three days. After three days, bring netting out into the light (hang from your pack) for an additional day or two and *keep moist*. Great with bacon bits.

CORINNE EDWARDS
WILLINGTON, CONNECTICUT

It's not impossible to have a fresh salad on the trail. I combine leaf lettuce, string beans, snow peas, and chopped herbs. I find that leaf lettuce will keep two to three days when rolled in paper towels and stored in a plastic bag. For dressing, I use leftover juice from sweet pickles.

JACK KONNER
BEAVERTON, OREGON

Nutritional information per serving

Depends upon the type of seeds used. Sprouts are generally a good source of vitamins A and C, protein, and calcium.

The Couscous Burrito of the Mighty San Gabriels

1½ cups couscous

1 package Lawry's Taco Seasoning

6 medium-size flour tortillas

6 hot sauce seasoning packages (or 3 teaspoons hot sauce)

3 ounces grated cheese

½ cups water per serving

Total weight: 1 pound 9 ounces
Weight per serving: 8.3 ounces
Total servings: 3 (2 burritos per serving)

At home:

Mix couscous together with taco seasoning and divide equally into three separate resealable plastic bags (about ½ cup each). Each bag represents one serving. Carry tortillas, hot sauce, and cheese separately. (Tortillas pack quite well against the back wall of your pack.)

On the trail:

For each serving, boil ½ cup of water in a pot. Add couscous-taco seasoning mix from one package. When hydrated, scoop onto two flour tortillas. Add one hot sauce packet per burrito along with some grated cheese.

This is one of my favorites. It's lightweight, easy to fix, has lots of carbohydrates, and is surprisingly hearty. The perfect meal!

KEVIN CORCORAN
PALMDALE, CALIFORNIA

Nutritional information per serving

calories	780
protein	21 g
carbohydrates	137 g
sodium	1,400 mg
fiber	13 g
fat	3 g
cholesterol	0 mg

Ozark Burritos

Total weight: 9 ounces
Total servings: 1 (2 burritos per serving)

1 (15-ounce) can kidney
beans
1 cup Pace Picanté Sauce
2 ounces cheddar cheese
2 wheat tortillas
1 cup water

At home:
Dry the kidney beans and picanté sauce in a food dehydrator. (Place the picanté sauce on plastic wrap to dry.) When dry, tear picanté leather into small pieces, and mix together with beans when dry. Package in a resealable plastic bag. Carry the cheese and tortillas separately.

On the trail:
Add picanté-bean mix to boiling water. Allow to cook until beans are fully rehydrated. The end product will be similar to refried beans. Spread the paste over two tortillas, sprinkle on the cheese, then roll up the tortillas like a burrito and eat from your hand. Other than the pot and a spoon, no plates, bowls, or other utensils are necessary.

CRAIG SMITH
"SMITTY"
SPRINGFIELD, MISSOURI

As vegetarians, our dinners all contained legumes. If we didn't have beans mixed in with our meals, we instead had split peas, miso, or lentil soup.

DAN AND SARA RUFNER
SAN DIEGO, CALIFORNIA

Nutritional information per serving

calories	930
protein	47 g
carbohydrates	151 g
sodium	3,690 mg
fiber	25 g
fat	25 g
cholesterol	60 mg

Joe's Way-Too-Exciting-for-Words Sandwiches

2 hamburger buns

2 slices Tillamook
Cheddar Cheese

4 slices of Hilshire Farms
Deli Select Ham

Total weight: 7 ounces
Total servings: 1

At home:
Package all items separately.

On the trail:
Add 1 slice of cheese and two slices of ham to each bun to make your sandwich. Hamburger buns actually hold up pretty well in the pack.

My advice would be to leave the stove at home! I did the whole Pacific Crest Trail without cooking, and I never missed it either. It was especially nice when it was raining (as it often does in the Cascades) to just get in the tent and eat a couple of sandwiches. You don't have to worry about fuel or doing dishes either. And you require less water, which is often scarce on the trail. Give it a try!

JOE SOBINOVSKY
CITRUS HEIGHTS, CALIFORNIA

Authors' note
Joe's recipe is included because it is so simple that most people do not think of it. In practice, many people wouldn't use it because hot food is such a large part of their whole outdoor experience. If you do give it a try on that next long trip, you obviously have to be very careful when carrying fresh meat. The salt and preservatives added during processing will help keep the lunch meat from spoiling, but the meat must also be kept cool and sealed to prevent bacteria from forming. This may be impossible in some trail environments and during warmer months. Use your head. If in doubt, don't risk making yourself ill.

Nutritional information per serving

calories	500
protein	29 g
carbohydrates	45 g
sodium	1,230 mg
fiber	2 g
fat	24 g
cholesterol	67 mg

Falafel Burgers

Total weight: 6 ounces
Total servings: 1

At home:

Mix falafel, onions, and Parmesan and store in a sealed bag. Carry oil and optional buns separately.

On the trail

Heat oil in frying pan. Mix falafel, onions, and Parmesan with water. Form into two burgers and flatten into pan. Cook over medium heat until browned on each side. Don't forget to flip them! Burgers can be placed on buns or English muffins or inside pitas. You may add whatever condiment topping you have in your pack: ketchup, mustard, relish, teriyaki sauce, or mayonnaise.

TIM AND CHRISTINE CONNERS
CINCINNATI, OHIO

---

4 ounces dried falafel

$\frac{1}{2}$ ounce dried onions

$\frac{1}{2}$ ounce Parmesan cheese (optional)

1 tablespoon oil

Just over $\frac{1}{3}$ cup water

Bread or buns (optional)

Nutritional information per serving:
(does not include bread)

calories	560
protein	21 g
carbohydrates	69 g
sodium	1,580 mg
fiber	13 g
fat	21 g
cholesterol	10 mg

Cottonwood Lakes Corn Macaroni

1 cup corn macaroni

⅛ teaspoon salt

1 envelope Schilling
   Instant Gravy Mix

½ cup unflavored TVP
   (textured vegetable
   protein)

2 cups cold water

Total weight: 6 ounces
Total servings: 1

At home:
Package all ingredients (except water) together in a resealable plastic bag. (Small corn macaroni will reconstitute more quickly than the large size.)

On the trail.
Place ingredients in a pot along with water and stir. Place pot on stove and simmer until macaroni is soft.

TVP can be ordered by mail through most food-supply catalogs or purchased from some of the larger markets with complete health-food sections. I also like to mix beef-flavored instant gravy with beef-flavored TVP and chicken-flavored instant gravy with chicken-flavored TVP. It tastes great, although the flavored TVP can be high in sodium.

IRWIN REEVES
BEAUMONT, CALIFORNIA

Nutritional information per serving

calories	480
protein	29 g
carbohydrates	73 g
sodium	1,500 mg
fiber	3 g
fat	5 g
cholesterol	0 mg

The Honeymooners' Cheesy Ramen

Total weight: 6 ounces
Total servings: 1

At home:
Package the ramen noodles and cheese separately.

On the trail:
Cook ramen noodles in boiling water until noodles are soft. Add ramen spice mix packet and stir. Cut cheese into pieces, add to noodles, and cook until it melts.

DAN AND TINA BREEDLOVE
"THE HONEYMOONERS"
EUDORA, KANSAS

1 large package ramen noodles, including spice packet

3 ounces cheese (your choice)

2 cups water

Nutritional information per serving

calories	640
protein	31 g
carbohydrates	61 g
sodium	1,080 mg
fiber	0 g
fat	30 g
cholesterol	29 mg

Doctari's Tuna Casserole

3 cups water

½ teaspoon salt

1½ cups basmati rice

2 6-ounce cans water-packed tuna, drained (or salmon)

1 (10¾-ounce) can of Campbell's Cream of Mushroom Soup

1 (15-ounce) can sweet peas, drained

1 (10-ounce) package frozen chopped broccoli

2 tablespoons dried parsley

1 (13.2-ounce) can mushrooms, chopped with juice

¼ cup shredded cheddar cheese

1 tablespoon cayenne (optional)

1½ cups water per serving

Total weight: 1 pound
Weight per serving: 4 ounces
Total servings: 4

At home:

Rinse and drain rice. In a large pot, bring 3 cups of water and the salt to a boil. Slowly add rice. Simmer covered for about 45 minutes or until tender. Add tuna, soup, peas, and broccoli. Stir and simmer for 5 minutes. Add parsley and mushrooms and simmer 10 additional minutes. Stir in cheese until melted. Line four dehydrating trays with plastic wrap. Place 2 cups of the casserole on each tray. Each tray represents one serving. When dry, store each serving in a 1-gallon resealable plastic bag.

On the trail:

For each serving, bring 1½ cups of water to a boil, then add one package of casserole. Stir frequently. For a bit more flavor, carry an extra can of tuna and add it toward the end of the cooking time.

GARY ADAMS
"DOCTARI"
CINCINNATI, OHIO

Nutritional information per serving

calories	510
protein	34 g
carbohydrates	73 g
sodium	1,890 mg
fiber	9 g
fat	10 g
cholesterol	42 mg

Forest Bulgur Pilaf

Total weight: 11 ounces
Weight per serving: 5.5 ounces
Total servings: 2

At home:
Dry carrots, potatoes, and zucchini in a food dehydrator. If you don't like the taste of sun-dried tomatoes, dry three Roma tomatoes and use these instead. Combine with powdered buttermilk and the remainder of the dry ingredients and package in a resealable plastic bag. Store Parmesan or Mrs. Dash separately.

On the trail:
Bring water to a boil. Add bagged vegetable mix. Simmer for 15 minutes or until bulgur is soft and water is absorbed. Remove from heat, and top with Parmesan cheese or Mrs. Dash if you like.

RON AND KAREN FOREST
MANITOU SPRINGS, COLORADO

$\frac{1}{4}$ cup finely chopped
carrots

$\frac{1}{4}$ cup finely chopped
potatoes

$\frac{1}{4}$ cup finely chopped
zucchini

6 sun-dried tomatoes,
chopped

2 tablespoons powdered
buttermilk

1 cup bulgur wheat

1 ($2\frac{1}{2}$-ounce) package
Knorr Fine Herb Soup
and Recipe Mix

Parmesan cheese or
extra-spicy Mrs. Dash
(optional)

$2\frac{1}{2}$ cups water

Nutritional information per serving

calories	640
protein	22 g
carbohydrates	114 g
sodium	1,580 mg
fiber	10 g
fat	9 g
cholesterol	6 mg

Sundown Sausage Delight

1 green bell pepper

1½ cups instant brown rice

9 sun-dried tomatoes, cut into small pieces

1 vegetable bouillon cube

2 bay leaves, cut into pieces

¼ teaspoon salt

½ teaspoon paprika

¼ teaspoon black pepper

⅛ teaspoon turmeric

½ teaspoon dried thyme

½ teaspoon dried oregano

½ teaspoon garlic powder

Cayenne (optional)

2 ounces smoked sausage

2¼ cups water

Total weight: 15 ounces
Weight per serving: 7.5 ounces
Total servings: 2

At home:

Chop bell pepper and dry in a food dehydrator. In a plastic bag, combine all dry ingredients. Pack sausage separately.

On the trail:

Cut sausage into small pieces. Bring water to a boil. Add rice mix and sausage to the water and return to a boil. Cover and cook over low heat until rice is tender.

CATHY CZACHOROWSKI
TORRINGTON, CONNECTICUT

Authors' note

Be sure to carry sausage that does not require refrigeration. Ensure that the open end of the sausage log does not spoil. An option to carrying one large stick of sausage on the trail is to carry several of the smaller sealed logs available through mail-order catalogs or your neighborhood Hickory Farms store.

Nutritional information per serving

calories	440
protein	13 g
carbohydrates	72 g
sodium	1,090 mg
fiber	5 g
fat	12 g
cholesterol	20 mg

Bear Ridge Scramble

Total weight: 1 pound 2 ounces
Weight per serving: 6 ounces
Total servings: 3

At home:

Package Nature Burger Mix in a resealable plastic bag. Carry tortillas and oil separately.

On the trail:

Add water to Nature Burger Mix and knead in the bag. Heat oil in pan. Add burger mix and scramble. Serve on tortillas. For variety, add fresh vegetables, cheese, salsa, meat, Parmesan cheese, or packages of ketchup, mayonnaise, or barbecue sauce.

Nature Burger mixes are nice but a pain to make as patties; but adding the water, scrambling it up in an oiled pan, and spreading it on tortillas—with whatever you find in your pack—is awesome. This recipe can easily be divided up into individual servings if desired.

DAN AND SARA RUFNER
SAN DIEGO, CALIFORNIA

I have found foods that might be too flavorful at home will barely be zesty enough on the trail, so I try to put a kick into my meals by adding spice. I like the Big Boy spice blend.

STEVE FUQUAY
"SWITCHBACK"
LAS VEGAS, NEVADA

1 package of Fantastic Foods Nature Burger Mix

6 medium-size whole-wheat tortillas

2 tablespoons canola oil

1½ cups water

Nutritional information per serving

calories	890
protein	24 g
carbohydrates	98 g
sodium	1,120 mg
fiber	14 g
fat	25 g
cholesterol	0 mg

Celebration Dinner

1 (6-ounce) slice smoked ham

3 cups frozen peas

6 ounces macaroni or egg noodles

1 cup grated Parmesan cheese

3 cups water

Total weight: 15 ounces
Weight per serving: 7.5 ounces
Total servings: 2

At home:
Cut ham into small pieces. Dry peas and ham thoroughly in a food dehydrator. Store together dried peas, ham, and noodles. Store Parmesan cheese separately.

On the trail:
Bring water to a boil. Add ham mixture and allow to cook until noodles are soft and meat is somewhat tender. Add Parmesan cheese.

This dinner is a real treat after a few weeks on the trail. We carry the ingredients and prepare it when we need to reward ourselves. It's easy to make and VERY tasty. Just the thing to lift your spirits when you feel dreary and without energy.

CHRIS WOODALL
SIMPSONVILLE, SOUTH CAROLINA

Nutritional information per serving

calories	780
protein	54 g
carbohydrates	86 g
sodium	2,210 mg
fiber	12 g
fat	20 g
cholesterol	165 mg

Ben's Chicken and Cheese

Total weight: 10 ounces
Weight per serving: 5 ounces
Total servings: 2

At home:

Break apart chicken and dry thoroughly in a food dehydrator. Store in a resealable plastic bag. In a separate resealable plastic bag, combine cheese-mix powder from macaroni dinner along with powdered buttermilk. Store noodles from the macaroni and butter separately.

On the trail:

Add a little water to the chicken and allow to rehydrate in bag. Bring a pot of water to a boil and add noodles. Cook until tender. Drain water, then add cheese sauce-buttermilk mix, butter, and rehydrated chicken. Allow to simmer until hot. Velveeta or dehydrated cheese can be substituted for the powdered cheese.

BEN YORK
ALPINE, CALIFORNIA

1 (5-ounce) can low-fat chicken (or water-packed tuna)

1 (7-ounce) package Kraft Macaroni and Cheese Dinner

2 tablespoons powdered buttermilk

1 tablespoon butter (or oil)

Water

Nutritional information per serving

calories	690
protein	34 g
carbohydrates	74 g
sodium	1,060 mg
fiber	2 g
fat	11 g
cholesterol	63 mg

Sweet Wenatchee Rice Dish

¼ cup raisins

½ cup diced dried apples

¼ teaspoon salt

½ teaspoon allspice

¼ cup low-fat powdered milk

½ cup chopped walnuts

1 cup instant brown rice

2 tablespoons margarine

1½ cups water

Total weight: 9 ounces
Total servings: 1

At home:
Mix together raisins, apples, salt, allspice, milk, walnuts, and rice and store in a 1-gallon resealable plastic bag. Pack margarine separately.

On the trail:
Bring water to a boil. Add rice mix and margarine. Stir, then let sit for about 5 minutes. Stir well.

This is a recipe that is simple to make, filling, and tastes great—perfect for backpacking. It is one of my favorites, and I never get tired of it. I used it a lot on the Pacific Crest Trail in 1983. I use the milk powder and nuts to help complete the protein, as this a meatless dish.

Lou Ann Fellows
Grand Canyon, Arizona

Nutritional information per serving

calories	1,200
protein	32 g
carbohydrates	141 g
sodium	1,150 mg
fiber	9 g
fat	62 g
cholesterol	8 mg

Bob 'n' Bug's Spanish Rice Fiesta

Total weight: 16 ounces
Weight per serving: 8 ounces
Total servings: 2

1 (16-ounce) jar Pace Thick and Chunky Salsa

2 cups instant dried refried beans

2 cups instant rice

Parmesan cheese or TVP (textured vegetable protein) (optional)

1 quart water

At home:

Dry salsa on plastic wrap in a food dehydrator. Tear salsa leather into pieces and store in a resealable plastic bag. Mix beans and rice together, along with optional TVP or dried cheese, and package in a separate resealable plastic bag.

On the trail:

Add salsa to water. Bring water to a boil while stirring to mix the salsa. Add rice-bean mix, stir, and remove from heat. Serve as a meal by itself or use flour tortillas to make burritos.

BOB AND JOY TURNER
"BOB 'N' BUG"
COEUR D'ALENE, IDAHO

Nutritional information per serving:
(does not include cheese and TVP)

calories	900
protein	32 g
carbohydrates	165 g
sodium	2,490 mg
fiber	28 g
fat	18 g
cholesterol	0 mg

Brown Rice Bonanza

2 cups frozen vegetable mix (corn, broccoli, bell pepper)

3 ounces chopped sun-dried tomatoes

1 cup instant brown rice

1 clove unpeeled garlic

3 condiment-size packets soy sauce (approximately 3 tablespoons)

1½ cups water

Total weight: 5 ounces
Total servings: 1

At home:
Dry frozen vegetables. Chop tomatoes. Add rice and unchopped garlic to vegetables and tomatoes. Store all ingredients and unopened soy-sauce packets together in a resealable plastic bag.

On the trail:
Bring water to a boil. Chop garlic and place all ingredients in the water; stir well. Cover the pan and remove from heat. Let stand 10 minutes. The vegetables need the time to rehydrate, as the rice will fully cook in 5 minutes. Pass out the soy sauce.

This rice-based dish is another recipe I regularly use.

CRAIG SMITH
"SMITTY"
SPRINGFIELD, MISSOURI

Nutritional information per serving

calories	750
protein	32 g
carbohydrates	149 g
sodium	2,810 mg
fiber	25 g
fat	5 g
cholesterol	0 mg

Quick-and-Not-So-Dirty Bean Soup and Rice

Total weight: 4 ounces
Total servings: 1

At home:
Place the contents of the dehydrated bean soup package and the rice and salt in a sandwich-size resealable plastic bag. Put the bagged contents back into the cup that the dehydrated soup was packaged in. (If you plan to have more than one Quick-and-Not-So-Dirty meal, place several cups one inside the other and put them into a 1-quart resealable plastic bag for protection.)

On the trail:
Empty the contents of the bag into the original packing cup. In a small pan, bring water to a rolling boil. Add the boiling water to the mix in the cup. Stir well and let stand for 6 minutes. The only thing you'll have to wash is the spoon. Use the resealable plastic bag as a trash container for the used hot cup.

This is one of my favorite recipes because it leaves no dirty dishes!

Emmett Autrey
"Ol Kooger"
Amarillo, Texas

1 (1.9-ounce) package
    Knorr Bean Soup Mix
    (black, navy, or Italian)
1 cup instant brown rice
$\frac{1}{8}$ teaspoon salt
1 cup water

Nutritional
information
per serving

calories	360
protein	14 g
carbohydrates	70 g
sodium	900 mg
fiber	11 g
fat	3 g
cholesterol	0 mg

Carolina Spice Rice

1 (3½-ounce) package
   Success Rice (boil-in-
   bag rice)

2 condiment-size packets
   soy sauce

1 small (2-ounce)
   pepperoni stick

1½ cups water

Total weight: 7 ounces
Total servings: 1

At home:
Carry rice, soy sauce, and pepperoni separately.

On the trail:
Boil the rice in water for about 10 minutes. Drain and pour cooked rice from bag into pot. Cut pepperoni stick into pieces and add to rice with soy sauce. Stir and it's ready.

JIM HOEFERLIN
CHARLOTTE, NORTH CAROLINA

Nutritional information per serving

calories	650
protein	21 g
carbohydrates	89 g
sodium	2,710 mg
fiber	1 g
fat	24 g
cholesterol	50 mg

Backpack Pot Pie

Total weight: 16 ounces
Weight per serving: 5.3 ounces
Total servings: 3

At home:

In a dehydrator, thoroughly dry chicken, mixed vegetables, and mushrooms. In a bowl, blend the dried chicken, vegetables, mushrooms, onions, garlic, Italian seasoning, parsley, buttermilk, and Cup-A-Soup mix. Divide mixture into three separate resealable plastic bags and label each "Chicken Pot Pie A."

In another bowl, combine Bisquick and the contents of second packet of Cup-A-Soup. Divide evenly into three separate bags and label each "Chicken Pot Pie B."

On the trail:

After you reach your camp, add ¼ cup water directly into Bag B and knead until it becomes a dough. Keep sealed. Next, pour the contents of Bag A into a pot along with water that covers the mix by 1 inch. Allow to sit for at least 30 minutes. While setting up your camp, check periodically to see if you need to add more water to keep the ingredients rehydrating. Once rehydrated, bring the contents of Bag A to a boil for about 2 minutes, making sure that the mixture doesn't dry out.

Reduce heat and pour the contents of Bag B on top of the contents of the pot. Either spoon the mixture on evenly and thinly or cut a hole at the bottom of the bag and squeeze the mix onto the chicken, being sure to smooth it out afterward. Cover and let simmer until Bisquick is cooked. Eat directly out of the pot.

Pam Coz-Hill
Visalia, California

Authors' note

We could not find Cream of Chicken dry soup mix at the grocery store. We were told by Lipton that it did exist but was hard to find. We substituted a broccoli and cheese soup mix, which worked well. To reduce sodium content, consider omitting the second packet of soup mix (found in Bag B).

Bag A:

2 (5-ounce) cans of light chunk chicken

1 (16-ounce) package frozen mixed vegetables

8 ounces sliced mushrooms

1 tablespoon dried minced onion

½ teaspoon granulated garlic

1 tablespoon Italian seasoning

1 teaspoon dried parsley

2 tablespoons powdered buttermilk

1 packet Cup-A-Soup Cream of Chicken (or Broccoli and Cheese)

Bag B:

2 cups Bisquick

1 packet Cup-A-Soup Cream of Chicken (or Broccoli and Cheese)

¼ cup water to add to Bag B

Nutritional information per serving

calories	630
protein	32 g
carbohydrates	88 g
sodium	2,290 mg
fiber	7 g
fat	16 g
cholesterol	70 mg

Adirondack Stew

1 bouillon cube

1 package Knorr Tomato
and Basil Soup Mix

¾ cup dried soup greens or
vegetable chips (or 16
ounces frozen mixed
vegetables,
dehydrated)

2 cups instant brown rice

1 tablespoon dried onion
flakes

1 tablespoon Italian
seasoning

1 teaspoon garlic powder

4 cups water

Total weight: 15 ounces
Weight per serving: 7.5 ounces
Total servings: 2

At home:

Mix all dry stew ingredients together and store in a
resealable plastic bag.

On the trail:

Bring water to a boil and add the stew mix. Boil 7 to
10 minutes until tender. Stir frequently.

Dried soup greens are usually available at the grocery store
in the spice section. Vegetable chips can usually be found
at a health food store.

WALT AND JANE DANIELS
MOHEGAN LAKE, NEW YORK

Nutritional information per serving

calories	670
protein	19 g
carbohydrates	133 g
sodium	1,990 mg
fiber	19 g
fat	7 g
cholesterol	0 mg

Cascade Stew

Total weight: 11 ounces
Weight per serving: 5.5 ounces
Total servings: 2

At home:

In a food dehydrator, dry the potatoes, carrots, and tomatoes. Dehydrate the dried beef even further; when stiff, break it up into small pieces. Mix all of these ingredients together with onion flakes and store in a resealable plastic bag. Carry potato flakes separately.

On the trail:

Add stew mixture to water and bring to a boil. Stir frequently. Let boil about 10 minutes or so until vegetables are fully rehydrated. Add potato flakes and stir.

ANN MARSHALL
PORT ORCHARD, WASHINGTON

1 pound potatoes, boiled and cut into small pieces

1 pound fresh carrots, boiled and cut

1 pound Roma tomatoes, cut into small pieces

1 (4½-ounce) jar Armour Sliced Dried Beef

3 tablespoons dried onion flakes

½ cup instant potato flakes

5 cups water

Nutritional information per serving

calories	570
protein	28 g
carbohydrates	104 g
sodium	3,170 mg
fiber	10 g
fat	5 g
cholesterol	50 mg

Oriental Takeout

1 pound shallots

1 pound bok choy

1 pound Asian eggplant

1 pound carrots

1 pound spinach

3 cups jasmine rice

3 ounces dried
mushrooms, chopped
small

4 ounces pork sung (or
chicken fu sung, beef
jerky, or ½ cup dried
beans)

2 (1-ounce packets) Noh
Oriental Stir-Fry
Seasoning

3 cups water per serving

Total weight: 2 pounds 4 ounces
Weight per serving: 9 ounces
Total servings: 4

At home:
Chop shallots, bok choy, eggplant, carrots, and spinach and dry in a food dehydrator. Once dry, combine with rice, mushrooms, pork sung, and stir-fry seasoning. Toss all ingredients together. Divide into four separate plastic bags of 3 cups each. Each bag represents one serving.

On the trail:
For each serving, bring 3 cups of water and the contents of one bag of ingredient mix to a boil. If using beans, add an additional ½ cup of water. Cook until rice is soft. Add more water if needed.

BENEDICT GO
"BEN GO"
VALLEJO, CALIFORNIA

Authors' note
Pork sung is a type of dried pork, and like several of the other ingredients for this recipe, will be found in Oriental food markets. It's well worth going out of your way, as this recipe is unique and delicious.

Nutritional information per serving:
(does not include pork sung)

calories	770
protein	22 g
carbohydrates	174 g
sodium	1,580 mg
fiber	13 g
fat	2 g
cholesterol	0 mg

Mountain Quesadilla

Total weight: 7 ounces
Total servings: 1

At home:

Dry mushrooms and onion in a food dehydrator. Dehydrate salsa on a dehydrator tray lined with plastic wrap. Once dehydrated, tear the salsa leather into tiny pieces and place in a sandwich-size resealable plastic bag along with the mushrooms and onion. Carry cheese, tortillas, and oil separately.

On the trail:

Add water to the salsa mixture and allow to sit for about 1 hour, adding additional dribbles of water if needed. Toss the water around in the bag frequently to help rehydrate. Once rehydrated, warm oil in pan on very low heat. Place one tortilla in pan. Pour salsa mix on top. Chop cheese into tiny pieces and place on top of this. Cover with the last tortilla. Brown each side until cheese melts. Wild onions can be used when available, as well as olives, tuna, canned chicken—whatever your tastes dictate and your backpack provides.

JOE AND CLAIRE HAGEMAN
"MONGOOSE AND BUTTERCUP"
TRENTON, NORTH CAROLINA

1 (7-ounce) can sliced mushrooms

1 medium onion, chopped

1 cup Pace Thick and Chunky Salsa

1 ounce provolone cheese

2 wheat tortillas

1 tablespoon olive oil

$\frac{1}{2}$ cup water

Nutritional information per serving

calories	640
protein	28 g
carbohydrates	81 g
sodium	2,640 mg
fiber	7 g
fat	34 g
cholesterol	25 mg

Curried Vegetable Couscous

1½ cups red lentils

7 cups water

3 tablespoons vegetable oil

1 cup finely chopped onion

1 fresh green chili pepper, minced

4 cups peeled and finely diced sweet potato

1 tablespoon mild curry powder

1 teaspoon ground cumin

2 tablespoons grated fresh gingerroot

4 cups diced cauliflower

2 cups diced green or red bell peppers

10 ounces diced fresh spinach

3 tablespoons fresh lemon juice

1 teaspoon salt (or to taste)

3½ cups couscous (or instant rice)

1½ cups water per serving to rehydrate

Total servings: 2 pounds 2 ounces
Weight per serving: 4.9 ounces
Total servings: 7

At home:

Rinse the lentils. In a large pot, bring 5 cups of water to a boil and add lentils. Reduce heat and simmer for about 30 minutes. In a separate large pan or wok, sauté the onion and chili pepper in oil for several minutes. Add sweet potatoes, curry powder, cumin, and ginger. Continue to sauté for 2 to 3 minutes. Add 2 cups of water along with cauliflower and bell peppers. Cover and simmer for 10 minutes or until cauliflower is tender. While the vegetables simmer, rinse and chop the spinach, removing the stems. Pour the lentils and their cooking liquid into a blender or food processor. Purée for 2 to 3 minutes. When cauliflower is tender, stir in the spinach, lentil purée, lemon juice, and salt. Simmer just until the spinach has wilted. Remove from heat.

Pour 1½ cups of vegetable mix onto plastic wrap on each of seven drying trays. Each tray holds the contents of one serving. Dehydrate. Once dried, place the contents of each tray in a separate resealable plastic bag. Add ½ cup couscous to each bag. Label each bag with the recipe's name and the amount of water required to reconstitute (1½ cups).

On the trail:

Bring 1½ cups water per serving to a boil. Add vegetable-couscous mix to the boiling water and heat until reconstituted (usually takes less than 5 minutes).

DEBBIE HIGGINS AND PETER SANDIFORD
"THE CANADIANS"
QUEBEC, CANADA

Nutritional information per serving

calories	600
protein	15 g
carbohydrates	109 g
sodium	410 mg
fiber	21 g
fat	8 g
cholesterol	0 mg

Beartown Couscous

Total weight: 1 pound
Weight per serving: 8 ounces
Total servings: 2

At home:

In a food dehydrator, dry carrots, onions, and bell pepper. Once dry, mix together and place in a 1-gallon resealable plastic bag. In another resealable plastic bag, package couscous, salt, sugar, and curry powder. (Couscous looks like millet but is actually a form of pasta, and it cooks much faster than spaghetti.)

On the trail:

Add vegetables to water and bring to a boil. When vegetables have rehydrated, add couscous mix and bring to a boil again. Remove from heat and let sit for a few minutes until couscous becomes soft. Add extra water if needed.

RICK BOMBACI
ENTERPRISE, OREGON

8 ounces sliced carrots, cooked

8 ounces diced onions

1 bell pepper, chopped

2 cups couscous

$\frac{1}{2}$ teaspoon salt

2 tablespoons brown sugar

2 tablespoons curry powder

$2\frac{1}{4}$ cups water

Nutritional information per serving

calories	840
protein	28 g
carbohydrates	174 g
sodium	1,250 mg
fiber	29 g
fat	5 g
cholesterol	0 mg

Italian Trail Couscous

1 (6-ounce) can tomato paste

1 cup couscous

3 tablespoons Parmesan cheese

1 teaspoon Italian seasoning

1 tablespoon olive oil (or your choice)

Salt to taste (optional)

1½ cups water

Total weight: 9 ounces
Total servings: 1

At home:
Dry the tomato paste on plastic wrap in a food dehydrator. Once dried, break tomato leather into small pieces and package along with couscous, Parmesan cheese, and Italian seasoning in a sandwich-size resealable plastic bag. Package oil separately.

On the trail:
Add all ingredients, as well as oil, to water. Let sit for 20 minutes. Bring to a boil, then reduce heat slightly and stir frequently. The cooking time depends on the altitude but normally takes about 3 minutes. When ready, the couscous should have the consistency of a moist paste.

This is a good and fast recipe. It's one of my classics. I eat it in the evening; and on some trips I have eaten it almost every day.

LUCA DE ALFARO
PALO ALTO, CALIFORNIA

Nutritional information per serving

calories	1,020
protein	43 g
carbohydrates	168 g
sodium	490 mg
fiber	11 g
fat	24 g
cholesterol	23 mg

Glazed Spam for Festive Occasions

Total weight: 15 ounces (including Spam can)
Total servings: 2

At home:
Package all ingredients separately.

On the trail:
Over medium heat, melt butter in pan. Add water and sugar slowly, stirring with your fork. Slice Spam into ¼-inch-thick cuts. Add Spam to pan, flipping once to allow both sides to brown. Don't let it burn!

TIM AND CHRISTINE CONNERS
CINCINNATI, OHIO

1 tablespoon butter

1 tablespoon water

¼ cup brown sugar

1 (12-ounce) can of Spam

A friend of mine had a recipe that caused envy among his fellow overnight hikers. He'd put a frozen steak in the top of his pack where it would keep his vegetables cool while it was thawing during the day. He'd then have a sizzling T-bone or ribeye and some fresh veggies for dinner while the rest ate that freeze-dried stuff. Of course, the steak had to be eaten the first day out.

VALERIE YORK
ALPINE, CALIFORNIA

Nutritional information per serving

calories	590
protein	21 g
carbohydrates	8 g
sodium	2,300 mg
fiber	0 g
fat	54 g
cholesterol	138 mg

Ground Beef Gravel

Lean ground beef

At home:

Cook lean ground beef thoroughly in a skillet. Use your favorite spices if desired. Pour off all accumulated grease. Rinse the cooked meat thoroughly with hot water in a kitchen strainer. Ensure that all clumps are broken up and that only very small pieces remain.

Next, place the meat on dehydrator trays and dry until hard. When it rattles like gravel, it will be finished. Allow to cool to room temperature. Cover with a lint-free cloth before storing in an airtight container or heavy-duty resealable plastic bag.

On the trail:

Cover beef gravel with water. It will rehydrate very quickly, usually within 5 minutes.

CRAIG SMITH
"SMITTY"
SPRINGFIELD, MISSOURI

Authors' note

This is a generic recipe for batch-drying ground beef for trail use. Dehydrate as much as you'll need for your upcoming trip, using it for whatever dishes you would normally add beef to. A little typically goes a long way.

Breads

Whole-Grain Trail Bread Mix

3 cups white flour

2 cups whole-wheat flour

½ cup wheat bran

1 cup wheat germ

2 tablespoons baking powder

1 teaspoon salt

½ cup powdered buttermilk

2 tablespoons margarine

For biscuits, dumplings, or pan bread: ⅓ cup water

For pancakes or tortillas: ½ cup water

Total weight (without margarine): 7 pounds 6 ounces
Weight per serving (without margarine): 1 pound 1 ounce
Margarine for frying: ½ ounce per tablespoon
Total servings: 7

At home:

Mix all dry ingredients, then divide and package into seven individual 1-cup servings. Store each in a separate sandwich-size resealable plastic bag. Carry margarine separately.

On the trail:

To make pan bread or biscuits: Melt 1 tablespoon of margarine in a pan. To one serving (one bag) of bread mix, add ⅓ cup water and 1 tablespoon margarine. Mix thoroughly. Either spoon out biscuit-size dough balls or pour entire bag of dough into a medium-hot frying pan. Cover pan until bread has risen some and is browned on one side. Flip and brown other side.

To make pancakes or tortillas: Melt 1 to 2 tablespoons of margarine in a pan. Add ½ cup of water, 1 tablespoon of margarine to 1 serving of bread mix (1 cup), in a resealable plastic bag. Mix. Pour onto greased medium hot fry pan, brown on one side. Turn over and brown the other side.

To make dumplings for soup: To one serving (one bag) of bread mix, add ⅓ cup water and 1 tablespoon margarine. Mix thoroughly. Drop by spoonfuls into bubbling soup. Cover and simmer for 2 minutes or until dumplings are thoroughly cooked.

This is a basic bread mix that can be used to make pan bread, pan biscuits, dumplings, pancakes, and tortillas.

KATHLEEN CUTSHALL
"THE OLD GRAY GOOSE"
CONNEAUT, OHIO

Nutritional information per serving:

(does not include margarine for frying)

calories	380
protein	16 g
carbohydrates	77 g
sodium	724 mg
fiber	7 g
fat	4 g
cholesterol	6 mg

Bulk-Building Bread-on-a-Branch

Total weight: 2 pounds 2 ounces
Weight per serving: 2.6 ounces
Total servings: 13

At home:
Mix all dry ingredients together and divide into thirteen individual sandwich-size resealable plastic bags of ½ cup of bread mix per bag.

On the trail:
Add ¼ cup water to one bag. Mix and knead the bag until the contents have the consistency of pie dough. Wrap dough along the peeled end of a branch in the form of a long, 6-inch blanket, and seal the end with a flap of dough. Hold over fire until golden brown. Slide or peel it off the stick to eat. (Note: It is better to use a small, live branch than a dead stick because the bread will slide off more easily once cooked.)

Caution: Be careful! Some shrubs and trees are poisonous, so exercise care when selecting a branch to use with this recipe. Know what you are doing and positively identify the safety of the tree or shrub from which the branch comes.

SANDY LEE BURNS
PROSPECT, OREGON

½ cup whole-wheat flour
½ cup barley flour
½ cup rye flour
½ cup oat flour
1 cup unbleached white flour
½ cup ground sesame seeds
½ cup whole sesame seeds
½ cup flax seeds
½ cup sunflower seeds
½ teaspoon salt
2 teaspoons baking powder
1 teaspoon baking soda
1½ cups powdered low-fat milk
½ cup ground rice or wheat germ
¼ cup water per serving

Nutritional information per serving

calories	230
protein	12 g
carbohydrates	26 g
sodium	270 mg
fiber	5 g
fat	11 g
cholesterol	4 mg

Chapatis
(Indian Herb Bread)

1 cup flour

½ teaspoon Italian
   seasoning

½ teaspoon salt

1 tablespoon olive oil

½ cup water

Total weight: 5 ounces
Total servings: 1

At home:
Place flour, Italian seasoning, and salt in a resealable plastic bag. Carry oil separately.

On the trail:
Add water to the contents of flour bag and knead well. *Important:* Let sit for at least 1 hour, then knead well again. Heat pan until hot, add oil, and roll dough very thin (about the thickness of two credit cards; you can use your water bottle as a roller and the bottom of a pot as a rolling surface). Place thin dough in pan and cook, flipping often, until brown spots appear. Do not overcook. This bread is excellent warm with a little peanut butter.

GARY ADAMS
"DOCTARI"
CINCINNATI, OHIO

I've baked while in the woods by placing a small pot on top of three small stones resting inside a larger pot. I've actually made pineapple upside-down cake, coffeecake, and corn bread using this method. All worked successfully, and each added a bit of cheer to the day.

RICK BOMBACI
ENTERPRISE, OREGON

Nutritional information per serving

calories	410
protein	12 g
carbohydrates	88 g
sodium	1,160 mg
fiber	0 g
fat	1 g
cholesterol	0 mg

The Canadians' Amazing Trapper's Bread

Makes 4 loaves (10 slices per loaf)
Weight per loaf: 2 pounds
Weight per serving: 3 ounces
Total servings: 40 (1 slice per serving)

At home:

Bring 2 quarts water to a boil and add raisins and currants. Cook for about 30 minutes (until raisins are plumped) before draining. In a large bowl, combine 2¾ cups hot water, brown sugar, salt, butter, and molasses. Stir until butter melts and cool the mix to lukewarm. Meanwhile, dissolve 2 tablespoons sugar in 1 cup of lukewarm (about 100°) water, then sprinkle dry yeast into the sugar-water mixture. Let stand for 10 minutes, then stir briskly with a fork. Add yeast-sugar-water mixture to butter-molasses mixture. Stir. Beat in 6 cups of all-purpose flour. Mix in plumped fruit, allowed to cool, with the remaining 6 cups of all-purpose flour. Blend by hand using a rotating motion.

Turn dough out on a lightly floured surface and knead for 8 to 10 minutes. Shape into a smooth ball and place in a greased bowl, rotating dough against the greased surface. Cover with a damp cloth and let rise in a warm place until doubled in bulk (approximately 2 hours). Punch down and shape into four loaves. Place loaves in four greased 8½x4½-inch loaf pans. Cover and let rise again until doubled (approximately 1 hour). Bake loaves simultaneously in an oven preheated to 375° for ½ to 1 hour, making sure that the bread doesn't burn. Brush tops with butter while hot.

Sliced thinly, this bread is suitable for drying, which will further prolong its storage life. A little water sprinkled on a slice while on the trail is all that is needed to rehydrate.

This bread will keep for two to three months without refrigeration. Also, the loaves freeze well, which preserves their life even longer. We tried experimenting with this recipe using whole-wheat instead of white flour and found that the bread wouldn't keep as long. We don't know why.

DEBBIE HIGGINS AND PETER SANDIFORD
"THE CANADIANS"
QUEBEC, CANADA

1½ cups raisins

1½ cups currants

2¾ cups hot water

1 cup lightly packed brown sugar

1 tablespoon salt

16 tablespoons (2 sticks) butter

1 cup molasses

2 tablespoons sugar

1 cup lukewarm water

2 tablespoons active dry yeast

12 cups all-purpose white flour

Nutritional information per serving

calories	210
protein	4 g
carbohydrates	28 g
sodium	100 mg
fiber	0 g
fat	10 g
cholesterol	51 mg

Table Mountain Orange Bread

2 cups whole-wheat flour

1½ cups white flour (or soy flour)

¾ cup sugar

2 teaspoons baking powder

½ teaspoon salt

¾ cup orange juice

½ cup low-fat milk

½ cup canola oil

1 egg

½ cup chopped dry-roasted mixed nuts

1 cup chopped Sun Maid Mixed Fruit

Makes 1 loaf (8 slices per loaf)
Total weight: 2 pounds 7 ounces
Weight per serving: 5 ounces
Total servings: 8 (1 slice per serving)

At home:

Preheat oven to 350°. Combine in large bowl the whole-wheat flour, white (or soy) flour, sugar, baking powder, and salt. Stir, then add orange juice, milk, oil, and egg. Mix until well blended, then add nuts and fruit. Pour into 8½x4½-inch greased loaf pan. Bake 65 minutes, or until a table knife inserted in the center comes out clean.

A planned 350-mile hike was cut short by problems with a pack string. To deal with the excessive leftovers, I developed this bread recipe as a way to use up my extra dried fruit and nuts. This bread packs well for weekend trips and is also suitable for drying. We have used it as Christmas gifts instead of conventional fruitcake, and folks are always pleased with it.

MARION DAVISON
APPLE VALLEY, CALIFORNIA

Nutritional information per serving

calories	510
protein	10 g
carbohydrates	75 g
sodium	330 mg
fiber	6 g
fat	20 g
cholesterol	28 mg

Swiss Alps Bread

Makes 4 loaves (8 slices per loaf)
Weight per loaf: 1 pound
Weight per serving: 2 ounces
Total servings: 32 (1 slice per serving)

At home:

Heat 2 cups of milk in a saucepan until scalded. Remove from heat. Add 1 cup sugar and all butter. Stir until butter melts.

In a small bowl, mix 1 teaspoon of flour, 1 teaspoon sugar, and 1 teaspoon of warm milk. Stir in package of yeast. Keep bowl in a warm place.

In a large bowl, beat eggs with vanilla. Add to this the scalded milk, the yeast mixture and the sifted flour. Stir well. Knead the bread dough on a floured board, adding more flour to the dough if required. Place in a greased bowl. Cover and let rise in a warm location for 2½ to 3 hours. Knead again. Cut and place in four greased loaf pans (8x3¾x2½-inch). Let rise for 1 hour. Preheat oven to 350° and bake for 45 minutes. Cover with aluminum foil if necessary to prevent burning. This bread may be dried to reduce weight and lengthen storage life.

Cathy Czachorowski
Torrington, Connecticut

---

2 cups milk

1 cup sugar

1½ cups butter (3 sticks) cold unsalted butter (*do not use margarine*)

1 teaspoon flour

1 teaspoon sugar

1 teaspoon warm milk

1 (¼-ounce) package Fleishmann's Rapid Rise Yeast

4 eggs

2 teaspoons vanilla

7½ cups sifted flour

Nutritional information per serving

calories	210
protein	4 g
carbohydrates	28 g
sodium	100 mg
fiber	0 g
fat	10 g
cholesterol	51 mg

Damper

1 cup low-fat powdered milk

1 individual package Butter Buds

2 cups self-rising flour

1 cup whole-wheat flour

Handful of raisins or dried fruit (optional)

½ cup water per loaf

Makes 2 loaves
Weight per loaf: 10 ounces
Weight per serving: 10 ounces
Total servings: 2 (1 loaf per serving)

At home:
Mix all dry ingredients together. Divide evenly into two separate resealable plastic bags (about 2 cups in each bag). Pack raisins separately.

On the trail:
Add ½ cup water to one bag. Knead ingredients into breadlike dough. No rising time is required. Remove mix and form into a ball. Bury the damper ball directly in the hot coals of a campfire. Wait about 20 to 30 minutes. The damper will rise like bread while cooking. Insert a thin stick into the ball to see if it is cooked through; if it extracts without traces of dough, the damper is finished. Remove the burnt exterior and eat the hot insides with butter or jam.

The damper ball can also be cooked in aluminum foil to reduce the burning of the crust. It can also be cooked in a pan with a lid or wrapped around a (nonpoisonous!) branch and cooked like a sausage-on-a-stick. In the latter case, it is best eaten with the left hand and your favorite drink in the right!

This adapted recipe was used by early settlers of Australia at every meal as a bread supplement. It is still cooked around campfires down under, particularly by Scouts. It tastes great with butter and jam.

GEOFF O'HARA
HONOLULU, HAWAII

Nutritional information per serving

calories	740
protein	32 g
carbohydrates	152 g
sodium	1,980 mg
fiber	7 g
fat	4 g
cholesterol	0 mg

Lazy Boy Roy's Biscuit-on-a-Stick

Total weight: 5 ounces
Weight per serving: 2.5 ounces
Total servings: 2

1 cup Bisquick
About ⅓ cup water

At home:
Pour Bisquick into a sandwich-size resealable plastic bag.

On the trail:
Add water to the bag, seal it, and knead it with your hands to make a stiff dough. Add dribbles of water to bring the dough to a moist, but not runny, texture. Bite or cut a little hole in the bottom corner of the bag, and squeeze the dough out onto the cooking stick, in candy-cane fashion while you slowly twirl the stick. (You can take the dough out of the bag to roll or shape it with your hands, but if you don't have any extra flour or oil in camp, this can get messy.) Make sure the dough is not too thick on the stick. Bake by turning the biscuit-on-a-stick over the campfire or coals slowly until golden brown.

Try adding Butter Buds, sugar, or powdered milk to the mix for variety. Also, see "Bulk-Building Bread-on-a-Branch" (page 115) for a more nutritious alternative.

Caution: As with the other bread recipes that use branches or sticks to cook the bread, ensure that the branch that you've selected does not come from a poisonous tree or shrub.

This is a campfire recipe. Like wieners-on-a-stick, it's super great for kids because they can do it themselves easily and safely; and it is really good.

ROY TRYON
CALIFORNIA CITY, CALIFORNIA

Nutritional information per serving

calories	255
protein	5 g
carbohydrates	38 g
sodium	740 mg
fiber	1 g
fat	9 g
cholesterol	0 mg

Pony Express Trail Bread

2 cups unbleached white flour

2 cups whole-wheat flour

$\frac{1}{3}$ cup wheat germ

3 tablespoons powdered low-fat milk

$\frac{3}{4}$ cup packed brown sugar

$1\frac{1}{2}$ teaspoons baking powder

$1\frac{1}{2}$ teaspoons salt

$\frac{3}{4}$ cup water

$\frac{1}{2}$ cup honey

$\frac{1}{2}$ cup molasses

$\frac{1}{3}$ cup vegetable oil

Total weight: 2 pounds 7 ounces
Weight per serving: 2.4 ounces
Total servings: 16 bars

At home:

Mix dry ingredients. Add and blend the rest of the ingredients until the dough mix is moist. Pour into a greased 8x8-inch or 9x9-inch square pan. Bake at 300° for 1 hour. The bread should pull away from the side of the pan when ready. Cut into squares while warm. Leave in pan to dry, uncovered, for 8 to 10 hours. Wrap individually in plastic wrap and store in resealable plastic bags. This bread keeps well when frozen and can be refrozen if not used. It also dries well in a dehydrator.

This bread packs beautifully. On one occasion, I took some out for a day ride on horseback and put it in the saddle bags. We had to come back early, and I forgot to take the bread out of the bags. Several days later, on another ride, we discovered the bread. We were over three hours from home and hungry, so we devoured it along with bruised apples and oranges. The bread fared far better than the fruit.

JEFF AND CHRIS WALL
LANCASTER, CALIFORNIA

Nutritional information per serving

calories	240
protein	4 g
carbohydrates	50 g
sodium	250 mg
fiber	2 g
fat	5 g
cholesterol	0 mg

Sutliff's Logan Bread

Makes 3 loaves (14 slices per loaf)
Total weight per loaf: 2 pounds 3 ounces
Weight per serving: 2.5 ounces
Total servings: 42 (1 slice per serving)

At home:

Mix together in a saucepan water, sugar, applesauce, molasses, honey, and margarine and bring to a boil, stirring. In a large bowl, blend together whole-wheat flour, white flour, baking soda, baking powder, cloves, and nutmeg. Pour in the liquid mixture, and stir well. Bake at 300° for 1 hour in three greased 9⅝ x5½x2¾-inch loaf pans (or five smaller 8½x4½x 2⅝-inch loaf pans). The bread will be considerably easier to slice if allowed to cool overnight. If you choose to dry this bread, the weight will be reduced to 2 ounces per slice.

1½ cups water
1¾ cups sugar
2 cups applesauce
½ cup molasses
⅔ cup honey
2 cups margarine
8 cups whole-wheat flour
2⅔ cups white flour
2 teaspoons baking soda
1 teaspoon baking powder
1 teaspoon ground cloves
1 teaspoon ground nutmeg

The name originated from an expedition in the 1950s to the region around Mount Logan on the Yukon-Alaskan border in the Saint Elias Range. The version of the recipe I use came to me twenty years ago from my friend Mary Sutliff, a guidebook author, horsewoman, former climber, and all-around mountain lady.

This bread carries very well. It will keep for at least two weeks in your pack, and if sliced and dried in your food drier, it will be light as a feather, hard as granite, and will keep forever (almost). The taste is something like a very substantial graham cracker. My partner and I dried several loaves of this bread for our Pacific Crest Trail trip. We stored it in resealable plastic bags and crammed it in our packs. Being dry, the slices cracked and broke, but the pieces were very tasty and served as a filler at mealtime.

ANN MARSHALL
PORT ORCHARD, WASHINGTON

(continued on next page)

Nutritional information per serving

calories	240
protein	4 g
carbohydrates	38 g
sodium	170 mg
fiber	3 g
fat	10 g
cholesterol	0 mg

(Sutliff's Logan Bread continued)

Authors' note

Dried Logan Bread has a flavor and texture similar to biscotti, dried cookie sticks often found in java shops for dipping in coffee. We made a very good trail version of biscotti by cutting each slice of Logan Bread in half lengthwise prior to drying. One gourmet option would be to add semisweet chocolate chips before baking. Then, when dipping your biscotti sticks, you'll be able to enjoy melted chocolate in your cowboy coffee while out on the trail. Roughing it? Hardly.

Whatever you do, use caution when biting down on dried Logan Bread. If you're not careful, you could lose a few teeth! In fact, its impressive physical properties probably make it useful for more than just sustenance. We wouldn't doubt that you could also use it to sharpen pocket knives or to build a fire ring!

Fuller Ridge Granola Fruit Muffins

Total weight: 12 ounces
Weight per serving: 1 ounce
Total servings: 12 (1 muffin per serving)

At Home:

Preheat oven to 425º. Combine in mixing bowl the flour, sugar, baking powder, salt, granola, and prunes. Add oil, egg, and milk. Stir until all ingredients are moist. Spoon into paper-lined or well-greased muffin pans. Bake 15 minutes. These freeze well and are great for weekend backpacking trips.

MARION DAVISON
APPLE VALLEY, CALIFORNIA

Authors' note:

These muffins make for a delicious resupply idea. Have a few sent to you at every stop on your long-distance treks!

1 cup whole-wheat flour

$\frac{1}{4}$ cup sugar

1 tablespoon baking powder

$\frac{1}{2}$ teaspoon salt

1 cup granola (or any type of oatmeal)

1 cup chopped prunes (or dried fruit of your choice)

3 tablespoons vegetable oil

1 egg, beaten

1 cup low-fat milk

I have discovered an indispensable tool for my cooking: a small plastic pot scraper. Many of my backpacking trips take place in the desert where water is scarce. I sometimes make dry camps far between water sources. The pot scraper can remove all the encrusted remains in the pot so that only a small splash of water is needed to finish the cleaning job.

PAM COZ-HILL
VISALIA, CALIFORNIA

Nutritional information per serving

calories	170
protein	4 g
carbohydrates	30 g
sodium	210 mg
fiber	2 g
fat	4 g
cholesterol	20 mg

Snacks and Desserts

Mountain Storm Chocolate Glop

1 tablespoon water

2 single-serving packages
  hot cocoa mix

1 tablespoon oil

Total weight: 2 ounces
Total servings: 1

On the trail:
Slowly mix water with cocoa mix into a thick blend. Stop adding water before the mixture becomes runny. Heat oil in pan. Add mixture to pan and fry. When it reaches the consistency of taffy, eat it straight from the pan.

I'll never forget the first time I had this. Christine and I were in a small lodgepole pine forest near timberline high in the Sierra. The first winter storm of the season was blowing in as Chris leisurely made our dessert following dinner. The chocolate glop really was a treat. However, I got stuck with cleanup duty, and with the sun long set and freezing rain stinging my face in gale-force winds, I scrubbed for what seemed like an eternity to get the sticky remnants out of my stainless steel pan. A couple of lessons on this one: (1) It tastes great. (2) Buy a nonstick pan before making it!

TIM AND CHRISTINE CONNERS
CINCINNATI, OHIO

Nutritional information per serving

calories	360
protein	2 g
carbohydrates	46 g
sodium	360 mg
fiber	1 g
fat	20 g
cholesterol	5 mg

Whitewater Cheesecake

Total weight: 1 pound
Weight per serving: 4 ounces
Total servings: 4

At home:

Remove the two pouches of cheesecake mix from the box. Pour the crust mix into a sandwich-size resealable plastic bag. Add the sugar. Pour the contents of the pouch containing the cheesecake mix into a 1-gallon resealable plastic bag and add the powdered milk. Carry the butter separately.

On the trail:

Add the butter (preferably warmed; you can place it in under your shirt on a cold evening to soften it) to the bag containing the crust mix. Knead the bag. Divide the crust mixture and pat it into the bottom of four individual cups.

To the bag containing the cheesecake mix, add cold water. (The water must be cold; otherwise the pudding mix may not congeal properly.) Knead bag to eliminate clumps in the mix, and then shake the bag for 3 minutes, ensuring that the seal stays tight. Cut a small hole at the bottom of the bag, and divide the cheesecake mix while squeezing it onto the crust of the four cups. Allow mix to jell, then eat right out of the cup.

Ed Acheson
Cincinnati, Ohio

1 (11-ounce) package Jell-O No-Bake Cheesecake

2 tablespoons sugar

$\frac{1}{8}$ cup low-fat powdered milk

5 tablespoons butter (optional)

$1\frac{1}{2}$ cups cold water

Nutritional information per serving

calories	330
protein	8 g
carbohydrates	60 g
sodium	590 mg
fiber	2 g
fat	8 g
cholesterol	8 mg

Clear Creek Cinnamon Chips

½ tablespoon cinnamon (or to taste)

2 tablespoons sugar (or to taste)

4 tablespoons vegetable oil

2 medium flour tortillas

Total weight: 9 ounces
Weight per serving: 4.5 ounces
Total servings: 2

At home:
Mix cinnamon with sugar and carry in a 1-gallon resealable plastic bag. Carry tortillas and vegetable oil separately.

On the trail:
Heat oil in frying pan. Cut tortillas into wedges. Place tortillas in hot oil and fry for a short period of time before flipping. Remove and let cool. Toss fried tortillas into the bag containing the cinnamon-sugar mix. Shake and eat straight out of the bag.

We fell in love on the Clear Creek Trail in the Southern Sierra's Piute Mountain Range. Worth naming a recipe after any day.

TIM AND CHRISTINE CONNERS
CINCINNATI, OHIO

Nutritional information per serving

calories	580
protein	5 g
carbohydrates	50 g
sodium	350 mg
fiber	3 g
fat	43 g
cholesterol	0 mg

Smitty's Apricot Brandy Flambé

Total weight (not including bottle weight): 7 ounces
Weight per serving: 3.5 ounces
Total servings: 2

At home:
Pack all ingredients separately.

On the trail:
In the morning, add fruit to the water in wide-mouth bottle and carry with you throughout the day. After the evening meal, pour off the water or drink it. Add brandy to the fruit, recap the bottle, and shake well for about 1 minute. Divide into two bowls and be sure to share the liquid equally (or your trail partner may complain!). Sprinkle sugar over the fruit.

Though this recipe is called a flambé, it would not be a good idea to set the liquid on fire for a couple of reasons: The brandy will evaporate and your plastic bowls will melt.

CRAIG SMITH
"SMITTY"
SPRINGFIELD, MISSOURI

1 cup dried apricots (or peaches or apples)

1 cup water (in wide-mouth plastic bottle)

¼ cup apricot brandy (or your favorite)

2 tablespoons sugar

Nutritional information per serving

calories	410
protein	3 g
carbohydrates	87 g
sodium	0 mg
fiber	6 g
fat	0 g
cholesterol	0 mg

Cache Peak Crumbles

1 cup Bisquick

¼ cup sugar (or more if you prefer)

⅓ cup canola oil

⅓ cup water

Total weight: 10 ounces
Weight per serving: 5 ounces
Total servings: 2

At home:
Mix Bisquick and sugar and store in a resealable plastic bag. Carry oil separately.

On the trail:
Heat oil in pan. Add water to Bisquick-sugar mix and knead in the bag. Pour mixture from bag into a heated pan and start scrambling like you would with scrambled eggs, trying to get all the mix covered with hot, greasy oil. Donut crumbles are ready when they are a little crispy. Be careful when eating directly from the pan because of the hot oil. Sweet, greasy donut crumbles—we aren't talking health food here!

If you have a few miles under your feet, a sweet tooth, and a little extra oil, it's definitely time for donuts! We named this recipe after a prominent peak northeast of the town of Tehachapi. On its eastern flanks, the Pacific Crest Trail fights its way through an aggressive defense of chaparral. It's incredibly beautiful, but rugged, country in which you can nearly see the scrub oak grow if you stop and watch. To us, Cache Peak stands as a reminder of the constant war to keep the trail clear of this spiky-leafed nuisance, and the Pacific Crest Trail Association has invested dozens of days and thousands of man-hours in keeping the trail passable in this area alone, not to mention throughout the remainder of Southern California.

When you see the name "Cache Peak," think of the efforts of the volunteers who make all the long trails possible. There are a hundred different battles currently being waged on your behalf, whether you are aware of them or not; and if you aren't among their ranks, the trail associations can certainly use your help.

TIM AND CHRISTINE CONNERS
CINCINNATI, OHIO

Nutritional information per serving

calories	560
protein	2 g
carbohydrates	86 g
sodium	370 mg
fiber	1 g
fat	42 g
cholesterol	0 mg

Mammoth Lakes Plop Cake

Total weight: 9 ounces
Weight per serving: 3 ounces
Total servings: 3

At home:

Mix together all dry ingredients. In three separate sandwich-size resealable plastic bags, place approximately ½ cup of mix in each.

On the trail:

Melt butter in pan over a low flame. Add 3 tablespoons of water to one bag of cake mix and knead inside the plastic bag. The mix should have a rather thick consistency. Plop a blob of cake mix into the pan, frying each side. When cooked through, add Deb and Marty's Mountain Lakes Trail Frosting (see next recipe).

When we received the recipe for frosting from Deb and Marty, we didn't have a trail cake recipe to go along with it. So we got busy, and plop cake was the result. This fun recipe gets its name from one of our favorite fun areas, the town of Mammoth Lakes and the Mammoth Mountain Ski Area. We have a lot of good memories from our times spent there.

Tim and Christine Conners
Cincinnati, Ohio

1 cup cake flour (or white flour)

¼ cup sugar

1 tablespoon powdered eggs

½ teaspoon baking soda

½ teaspoon baking powder

3 tablespoons water per serving

1 tablespoon butter per serving

Nutritional information per serving

calories	310
protein	4 g
carbohydrates	143 g
sodium	370 mg
fiber	0 g
fat	11 g
cholesterol	35 mg

Mountain Lakes Trail Frosting

1½ teaspoons powdered buttermilk

5 tablespoons powdered sugar

1 teaspoon cake flour (or white flour)

1 single-serving package hot chocolate mix (or 5 teaspoons of any pudding mix)

1 teaspoon squeeze margarine per serving

2 teaspoons water per serving

Total weight: 3 ounces
Weight per serving: 1 ounce
Total servings: 3

At home:

Mix together all dry ingredients. In each of three separate resealable plastic bags, place approximately 3 tablespoons of mix. Store margarine separately.

On the trail:

Add 1 teaspoon margarine and 2 teaspoons water to one package of frosting mix, kneading within the package. Pour onto cake or other dessert.

DEBORAH BRILL
SCOTT "MARTY" PLACE
BERKELEY, CALIFORNIA

Nutritional information per serving

calories	130
protein	1 g
carbohydrates	24 g
sodium	81 mg
fiber	0 g
fat	4 g
cholesterol	1 mg

Decadence Chocolate Pie

Total weight: 11 ounces
Weight per serving: 2¾ ounces
Total servings: 4

At home:
Crush Oreos and place them in a resealable plastic bag along with the chocolate sprinkles. In another resealable plastic bag, mix the chocolate pudding mix and powdered milk.

On the trail:
Add cold water to the bag containing the pudding mix and shake vigorously for 2 to 3 minutes. Be absolutely sure that the bag is zipped shut! Divide the contents into four equal servings, then sprinkle the crushed cookies and the chocolate sprinkles over the puddings.

Craig Smith
"Smitty"
Springfield, Missouri

Authors' note
Is it possible to have decadent food while on the trail? If your answer is no, try this recipe. You might just change your mind.

8 Oreo cookies

1 tablespoon chocolate sprinkles

1 (6-ounce) package Jell-O Instant Chocolate Pudding

½ cup low-fat powdered milk

1½ cups cold water

Nutritional information per serving

calories	290
protein	5 g
carbohydrates	57 g
sodium	750 mg
fiber	1 g
fat	5 g
cholesterol	4 mg

Hanging-by-Your-Boots Upside-Down Cake

4 slices dried pineapple

1 cup biscuit mix

1 tablespoon sugar

4 tablespoons brown sugar

$\frac{1}{4}$ cup water (to prepare cake mix)

1 cup boiling water (to rehydrate pineapple)

1 toothpick (or a knife)

Total weight: 10 ounces
Weight per serving: 2.5 ounces
Total servings: 4

At home:
Cut dried pineapple into ¼-inch chunks, and store in a resealable plastic bag. In a separate 1-gallon resealable plastic bag, mix together biscuit mix and white sugar. Store brown sugar separately.

On the trail:
Add ¼ cup water to biscuit mix and knead in bag. Set aside. Boil 1 cup water and pour into a small container. Add pineapple. Let fruit rehydrate while dinner is cooking, waiting at least 20 minutes. Put rehydrated pineapple and its liquid in a pot and boil slowly for 10 minutes. Sprinkle brown sugar on top of pineapple, and do not stir. Lower heat. Drop dough by the spoonful onto pineapple and allow batter to spread. (The dough will be gooey with a consistency somewhere between biscuit and pancake mix.) Do not disturb the pineapple bottom. Cover and steam for about 10 minutes. When a toothpick or knife inserted in the center comes out clean, it's time for cake.

Possible replacements for the pineapple:

30 dried apricots cut into small strips. Add 2 tablespoons sugar while rehydrating.

1 cup mixed dried-fruit bits. Add 1 tablespoon sugar while rehydrating.

WALT AND JANE DANIELS
MOHEGAN LAKE, NEW YORK

Nutritional information per serving

calories	200
protein	3 g
carbohydrates	36 g
sodium	370 mg
fiber	1 g
fat	5 g
cholesterol	0 mg

Sunset Bagel

Total weight: 4 ounces
Total servings: 1

1 bagel

1 tablespoon butter

On the trail:

Cut bagel in half. Place ½ tablespoon butter on each side and fry in pan until toasted. It doesn't get much easier than this!

With nearly every dinner, I finished up with a toasted bagel. I would butter one half of the bagel and cook it briefly, using the pot lid as a frying pan. It was quick, delicious, and the envy of all.

RICK BOMBACI
ENTERPRISE, OREGON

Nutritional information per serving

calories	360
protein	10 g
carbohydrates	51 g
sodium	580 mg
fiber	3 g
fat	12 g
cholesterol	30 mg

Crabtree Tragedy Pudding

1 (5-ounce) package Jell-O Instant Vanilla Pudding (or other flavor)

½ cup low-fat powdered milk

2 cups cold water

1 container with sealing lid (a wide-mouth drinking bottle works well)

Total weight: 6 ounces
Weight per serving: 3 ounces
Total servings: 2

At home:
Package all ingredients separately.

On the trail:
Place all three ingredients in a wide-mouth container. Close lid securely and shake vigorously until thickened. This usually takes 1 to 2 minutes, depending on the temperature of the water. Container can be placed in a cold lake or stream to help chill.

A friend of mine named Whiteroot tried to copy this recipe at Crabtree Meadow. He used regular pudding instead of instant and, as a result, shook and shook the mix for hours with no results.

DIANE KING
SOMERS, CONNECTICUT

Authors' note
If you've ever been deep in the wilderness for days on end, you can appreciate the magnitude of Whiteroot's tragedy! For crying out loud, always remember him and use instant, man! Dan and Sara Rufner suggest you try this type of pudding with vanilla wafers or animal cookies, especially when using vanilla-flavored mix.

Nutritional information per serving

calories	410
protein	14 g
carbohydrates	86 g
sodium	1,190 mg
fiber	0 g
fat	2 g
cholesterol	15 mg

Chocolate-Coated Banana Chips

Total weight: 4.5 ounces
Total servings: 1

At home:
Mix together all dry ingredients and store in a resealable plastic bag. Carry oil separately.

On the trail:
Heat oil in frying pan. Add banana-chocolate mix and fry until chocolate melts. If using cocoa mix instead of chocolate chips, add 1 or 2 teaspoons of water. Be careful that the mixture doesn't burn. Eat out of the pan hot or let cool first.

A resupply variation: Use fresh bananas, split and sprinkle with nuts and chocolate chips, wrap in aluminum foil, and place on glowing coals until hot and gloppy.

CHET J. FROMM
PORT ORANGE, FLORIDA

$\frac{1}{2}$ cup banana chips

$\frac{1}{4}$ cup walnuts

$\frac{1}{4}$ cup chocolate chips (or a package of cocoa mix)

2 tablespoons vegetable oil

Water (optional)

Nutritional information per serving

calories	850
protein	8 g
carbohydrates	50 g
sodium	30 mg
fiber	1 g
fat	53 g
cholesterol	0 mg

Buried Forest Trail Fudge

4 large marshmallows

2 tablespoons powdered buttermilk (or powdered milk)

3 tablespoons brown sugar

½ cup oatmeal (or 1 single-serving package instant oatmeal)

3 tablespoons hot chocolate mix (or 1 single-serving package)

¼ cup M&Ms

3 tablespoons margarine

2 tablespoons chunky peanut butter

3 tablespoons water

Total weight: 10 ounces
Weight per serving: 5 ounces
Total servings: 2

At home:
Cut marshmallows into small pieces and store in a resealable plastic bag. Combine buttermilk, sugar, oatmeal, hot chocolate, and M&Ms in a resealable plastic bag. In separate containers, store peanut butter and margarine (a squeeze bottle is convenient to carry).

On the trail:
Over a low flame using a nonstick pan, heat margarine, peanut butter, and marshmallows until melted. Add the rest of the ingredients, including water, and mix until a soft fudge. Eat hot right out of the pan.

This dessert is made from ingredients normally found left over in one's pack prior to resupply. It will have the consistency of thick oatmeal and should be eaten with a spoon.

DEBORAH BRILL
SCOTT "MARTY" PLACE
BERKELEY, CALIFORNIA

Nutritional information per serving

calories	700
protein	11 g
carbohydrates	92 g
sodium	430 mg
fiber	4 g
fat	32 g
cholesterol	8 mg

Goat Rock Fudge

Total weight: 2 pounds
Weight per serving: 1.3 ounces
Total servings: 24 (1 bar per serving)

$\frac{2}{3}$ cup milk (or more for a creamier taste)

2 cups sugar

$\frac{3}{4}$ cup mini marshmallows

2 cups chunky peanut butter

$\frac{1}{2}$ cup plain M&Ms

At home:

Add milk to sugar in a 2-quart pot. Cook over medium heat until mixture comes to a boil, then simmer for 3 to 5 minutes. Remove from heat, and quickly add marshmallows, peanut butter, and M&Ms. Allow chocolate to melt, then mix and pour into a 10x7-inch greased pan. Allow to cool. Cut when firm, then package for the trail.

KEVIN HOBART
"BLUE"
MOUNT VERNON, WASHINGTON

Nutritional information per serving

calories	210
protein	6 g
carbohydrates	25 g
sodium	110 mg
fiber	2 g
fat	12 g
cholesterol	1 mg

Peanut Butter Fudge

1½ cup quick oats

1 (14-ounce) can Eagle Brand Sweetened Condensed Milk

½ teaspoon salt

1 teaspoon vanilla extract

½ cup chunky peanut butter

1 (12-ounce) bag semisweet chocolate chips

Total weight: 2 pounds 1 ounce
Weight per serving: 2.1 ounces
Total servings: 16 (1 bar per serving)

At home:

Preheat oven to 350°. Combine oats, condensed milk, salt, and vanilla. Stir in the peanut butter and chocolate chips. Press into 8-inch-square greased baking pan. Bake for 30 minutes. Cool, cut, and pack in snack-size resealable plastic bags.

MARION DAVISON
APPLE VALLEY, CALIFORNIA

Nutritional information per serving

calories	260
protein	5 g
carbohydrates	35 g
sodium	140 mg
fiber	1 g
fat	12 g
cholesterol	6 mg

Gonky Balls

Total weight: 2 pounds 3 ounces
Weight per serving: 1.4 ounces
Total servings: 25 (1 ball per serving)

At home:

Melt butter in saucepan and stir in milk and sugar.
Bring to a boil and add vanilla. Stir in remaining
ingredients. Let cool until mixture becomes sticky,
then roll into 25 balls, each 1 inch in diameter.

DEBBIE HIGGINS AND PETER SANDIFORD
"THE CANADIANS"
QUEBEC, CANADA

8 tablespoons (1 stick)
   butter

½ cup low-fat milk

2 cups sugar

1 teaspoon vanilla

3 cups quick oats

1 cup shredded
   sweetened coconut

2 tablespoons cocoa
   powder

**Nutritional
information
per serving**

calories	110
protein	2 g
carbohydrates	24 g
sodium	40 mg
fiber	2 g
fat	6 g
cholesterol	12 mg

Fuel Fudge

1 16-ounce jar of creamy peanut butter

4 ounces hot bacon grease, strained (or 1 cup lard)

$\frac{1}{2}$ cup honey

3 cups powdered milk

2 cups crushed peanuts

1 cup raisins

1 cup flaked sweetened coconut

Total weight: 1 pound 5 ounces
Weight per serving: 0.7 ounce
Total servings: 32 (1 bar per serving)

At home:

Microwave the jar of peanut butter on high for 1 minute or until it flows easily. Plop peanut butter into a mixing bowl. Stir in bacon grease. Next, mix in honey, powdered milk, peanuts, raisins, and coconut. Spread 1-inch thick in two greased 8x8-inch pans and let cool. Cut the contents of each pan into 16 squares and store in resealable plastic bags.

It may turn a bit gloppy after a couple of weeks on the trail, but it will still be very good. It should keep unspoiled for about four weeks with no problem, but you will eat it all before then anyway.

This recipe is very, very rich and not for normal recreational eating. We take a small amount when we really need energy. During a very long strenuous ascent late in the day, when you need to make a few more miles, or on a cold night before getting into your bag, that's when it is effective. I got the idea for this recipe one night in Maine when a fellow hiker related how he ate pure butter or grease before he went to sleep in cold weather in order to keep warm during the night. This is my variation on his idea. Long-distance backpacking is the only activity to warrant this high calorie stuff!

JOHN WOODALL
SIMPSONVILLE, SOUTH CAROLINA

Nutritional information per serving

calories	250
protein	9 g
carbohydrates	19 g
sodium	110 mg
fiber	3 g
fat	19 g
cholesterol	6 mg

Watermelon Candy

Total weight: 1 ounce
Total servings: 1

1 pound fresh cut
watermelon

At home:
Dehydrate watermelon for the best candy around!
Package for the trail.

Dan and Sara Rufner
San Diego, California

Know the capabilities of your pack stove. Once we tried a new cooking method on an old stove that had the fuel container just below the flame. After the stove had been operating at a high setting for about twenty minutes, the fuel began to boil and then the stove exploded! The whole trip was ruined, but, thankfully, nobody was hurt. On another occasion, the breeze blew the heat away from an already underpowered stove, and it took forever to prepare the meal.

Jeffrey Hare
Citrus Heights, California

Nutritional information per serving

calories	140
protein	3 g
carbohydrates	32 g
sodium	20 mg
fiber	2 g
fat	2 g
cholesterol	0 mg

Yellow Worms

1 tablespoon all-purpose flour

1 rounded tablespoon lemonade powder (or lemon sports-drink powder, or ½ tablespoon lemon juice or lemon peel shavings)

1 package ramen noodles (without seasoning packet)

2 tablespoons water

Total weight: 4 ounces
Total servings: 1

At home:
In a resealable plastic bag, combine flour and lemon powder. Carry noodles separately.

On the trail:
Boil and drain noodles. Add water to lemon powder bag and mix the contents. Pour lemon-flour mix over noodles and toss. Save some hot water to clean the sticky spoon when you're done.

WILL O'DAIX
"THE GREEN GHOST"
INDIANAPOLIS, INDIANA

Authors' note
Yellow worms may be an acquired taste—that is, acquired after being on the trail too long! The flavor is creamy bittersweet and certainly very unique. But, who knows: It may be just what you need when you're craving carbohydrates and sugar. It's easy, so give it a try.

Nutritional information per serving

calories	390
protein	10 g
carbohydrates	80 g
sodium	670 mg
fiber	0 g
fat	3 g
cholesterol	0 mg

Rocky Fork Fruit Leather

Total weight: 4 ounces
Weight per serving: 2 ounces
Total servings: 2 (1 roll per serving)

1 quart fruit (fresh, frozen
and thawed, or
drained canned)

1 tablespoon lemon juice

At home:

Purée your favorite fruit in a blender. Add lemon juice. Cover two inverted baking sheets with heat-resistant plastic wrap. Pour purée over each baking sheet to a depth of about ¼ inch. Leave a 1-inch border around the edge. Dry in the oven at 140° until purée becomes leathery, not sticky, and still pliable. This will take anywhere from 5 to 10 hours. Roll the fruit leather up and store in an airtight container or bag.

I named this recipe after my childhood stomping grounds. My folks had a small plot of land and a trailer out in the countryside of southern Ohio near Rocky Fork Lake. We would often go there to get away from the city. It was there that I developed a love for the outdoors and for the open spaces. Life was simple at Rocky Fork. Perhaps because of this simplicity, it was a wonderful place for family to gather together undistracted, concentrating instead on fun and fellowship around the campfire.

It's been many years since I've been to Rocky Fork. The land has long been sold. Having recently returned to Ohio after living in California for quite some time, I was happy to learn that the North Country National Scenic Trail passes near the Rocky Fork region. It is a strong excuse to return to that area and pick up where I left off as a child.

—Tim

Tim and Christine Conners
Cincinnati, Ohio

Nutritional information per serving

(Values will vary depending on the type of fruit you use. Following are two examples.)

One serving of fruit rolls made from fresh peaches:

calories	300
protein	5 g
carbohydrates	77 g
sodium	10 mg
fiber	11 g
fat	1 g
cholesterol	0 mg

One serving of fruit rolls made from fresh strawberries:

calories	180
protein	4 g
carbohydrates	43 g
sodium	4 mg
fiber	16 g
fat	2 g
cholesterol	0 mg

Secret-to-Success Cookies

1 pound (4 sticks) margarine

3 eggs

1½ cups white sugar

1¼ cups dark brown sugar

4 teaspoons vanilla

3 cups flour

4 teaspoons baking powder

4 teaspoons cinnamon

1 cup wheat bran

3 cups oats

1¼ cups walnuts, chopped

3 cups semisweet chocolate chips (or raisins if you prefer)

Total weight: 4 pounds 12 ounces
Weight per serving: 0.6 ounce
Total servings: 120 (1 cookie per serving)

At home:

Preheat oven to 350°. Mix all ingredients together with an electric beater in a very large bowl. If the dough is too runny, add more oats. Drop teaspoon-size balls on greased baking sheets. Bake for 10 to 12 minutes.

These cookies were my secret to success. I baked a few thousand of these cookies before both of my hikes on the Appalachian Trail and the Pacific Crest Trail. I froze them and had them sent to me in my food-supply packages. They were a very satisfying treat after dinner, a gift to myself for hiking hard. I found them also to be a very valuable commodity on the trail, useful as money, gifts, or just a nice way to make someone happy.

ALLMUTH PERZEL
"CURLY"
TOLLAND, CONNECTICUT

Nutritional information per serving

calories	80
protein	2 g
carbohydrates	13 g
sodium	30 mg
fiber	1 g
fat	3 g
cholesterol	6 mg

Cascade Carob-Seed Candy

Total weight: 1 pound 6 ounces
Weight per serving: 1 ounce
Total servings: 24

At home:

Mix together dry ingredients, then add honey and peanut butter. The mixture will be stiff and will require much kneading with a wooden spoon or your hands. Heat briefly in the microwave if the mixture is too stiff. Form into 24 quarter-size balls. Package and refrigerate until ready to hike.

MARION DAVISON
APPLE VALLEY, CALIFORNIA

$\frac{1}{2}$ cup carob powder

$\frac{1}{4}$ cup wheat germ

$\frac{1}{4}$ cup soy flour

$\frac{1}{2}$ cup unsalted sunflower seeds

$\frac{1}{2}$ cup sesame seeds

$\frac{1}{2}$ teaspoon salt

$\frac{1}{2}$ cup honey

$\frac{1}{2}$ cup chunky peanut butter

Nutritional information per serving

calories	105
protein	4 g
carbohydrates	11 g
sodium	80 mg
fiber	2 g
fat	6 g
cholesterol	0 mg

Campin' Candy Bars

½ cup dates, chopped

1 cup apricots, chopped

1 cup yellow raisins

½ cup sweetened
    shredded coconut

1½ cups Rice Krispies

½ cup low-fat granola

½ cup wheat germ

½ cup unsalted sunflower
    seeds

½ cup unsalted sesame
    seeds

½ cup cashews, chopped
    and salted

2 (12-ounce) packages
    milk-chocolate chips

2 (6-ounce) packages
    butterscotch chips

½ cup honey

Total weight: 4 pounds 5 ounces
Weight per serving: 2.2 ounces
Total servings: 32 (1 bar per serving)

At home:

In a large bowl, mix together dry ingredients, except chips. Melt chocolate and butterscotch chips in a double boiler (or microwave) and add honey. Blend chocolate-butterscotch mixture with dry ingredients, stirring well. Reheat in microwave to soften if mixture becomes too stiff. Pour onto greased 10¼x15¼-inch sheet. Cool and then cut into 32 squares. Wrap in plastic wrap and store in freezer or refrigerator until ready to hit the trail.

Jane and Walt Daniels
Mohegan Lake, New York

Nutritional information per serving

calories	270
protein	4 g
carbohydrates	38 g
sodium	70 mg
fiber	2 g
fat	14 g
cholesterol	6 mg

Snacks for Trail Dogs

Total weight: 9 pounds 4 ounces
Weight per serving: 1.5 ounces
Total servings: 100 (1 biscuit per serving)

At home:

Soak oats, rice, barley, rye, rolled wheat, millet, corn-meal, triticale, and mixed beans overnight in vegetable broth. The following day, add the powdered milk to the soaked ingredients and cook until beans are soft. Take kettle off stove and stir in remaining ingredients with a wooden spoon. The mix will be very thick and heavy.

Pat out mixture ½-inch thick onto four 10¼x15¼-inch cookie sheets. Score into 3x3-inch squares. Dry in a warm oven at 175° for about 8 hours or until dry. Package any way that is most convenient for you.

CHUCK AND SUSAN ATKINSON
DORRIS, CALIFORNIA

One day, while hiking along the Pacific Crest Trail with my trail dog, Bernadette, and my faithful pack llama, Dancing Cloud, I met a man named Chuck Atkinson out with his bright-eyed, happy dog. While discussing trail conditions, I immediately took note of how perky and alert his dog appeared. My dog, on the other hand, seemed glum and sore footed; and so I asked him what his secret was. He explained how he and his wife, Susan, make their own healthy pack food for themselves as well as for their obviously healthy dog. So I inquired what I could do for my "dying-on-the-vine" young pup. He seemed delighted to take his valuable prime hiking time to do so, and I was ready with pen in hand to record it.

(continued on next page)

2 cups rolled oats

2 cups rice

2 cups rolled barley

2 cups rolled rye

2 cups rolled wheat

2 cups millet

2 cups cornmeal

2 cups rolled triticale

1 (16-ounce) can of mixed beans

4 quarts of vegetable broth (made without potatoes)

3 cups low-fat powdered milk

2 tablespoons salt

15 crushed kelp tablets (or capsules)

1 cup of garlic powder

1 cup oregano

$\frac{1}{3}$ cup bonemeal

1 cup shredded carrots

2 cups corn oil (or olive oil)

6 cups whole-wheat flour

Nutritional information per serving

calories	150
protein	5 g
carbohydrates	24 g
sodium	210 mg
fiber	4 g
fat	5 g
cholesterol	1 mg

(Snacks for Trail Dogs continued)

I went home after that week-long pack trip, and made these doggie biscuits for my dog. She was able to travel the remainder of the summer over 400 continuous miles without sore feet and was peppy every step. I ate some, too, and they are delicious! To Chuck and Susan's recipe, I add ½ cup ground sesame seed, ½ cup ground flax, ½ cup pumpkin seed, and ½ cup sunflower seed, which I believe are good for eliminating worms in dogs.

SANDY LEE BURNS
PROSPECT, OREGON

The Atkinson's note:

We feed our dogs two biscuits three times per day per dog. Added to this, our black lab, Wolfie, and our coyote-husky mix, Wilie, nibble on our gorp and whatever we do not eat.

Why the special food? It certainly helps when out on the trail to feed the animals a quality food on a day-to-day basis. We start feeding the dogs high-quality dog food two weeks before a long trek starts. This gets them physically ready for the trip and prepares their stomachs for the very nutritious trail food that they will eat. If your dogs eat cheap food before a long trek, be aware that their stomachs will be larger because they have to eat more food to overcome the junk that's in it.

Our dogs are an integral part of our backpacking. They are very protective of our campsite. Wilie has acutely sensitive ears and lets us know when others are on the trail or if there is something close by worth noting. Wolfie seems to have a second sense about him for finding water for us. Both dogs have their own packs, allowing them to each carry their own water and food.

Super-Duper Mega Rice Krispie Treat

Total weight: 1 pound 5 ounces
Weight per serving: 0.9 ounce
Total servings: 24 (1 bar per serving)

At home:

Place margarine in a large microwave-safe bowl and melt in the microwave (about 45 seconds). Add marshmallows; microwave until melted (about 90 seconds). Stir in Rice Krispies. Add cashews and cranberries. Oil up your hands with shortening, then grease a 15¼x10¼x¾-inch pan; if you are doubling the recipe, spread wax paper over a large surface. Remove mixture from bowl and press out flat. Heat as needed to keep the mixture soft. Cut into 24 squares. Wrap in plastic or store in resealable plastic bags.

My last Super-Duper Mega Rice Krispie Treat was 5 square feet and made for a nice conversation piece.

CRAIG GIFFEN
PORTLAND, OREGON

¼ cup margarine

40 large marshmallows

6 cups Rice Krispies

1 cup unsalted raw cashews

1 cup Ocean Spray Craisins (or dried cranberries)

1 tablespoon shortening

Peanuts, oatmeal, raisins (optional)

Nutritional information per serving

calories	110
protein	1 g
carbohydrates	16 g
sodium	30 mg
fiber	1 g
fat	5 g
cholesterol	0 mg

Drinks

Border-to-Border Berry Milk Shake

1 (16-ounce) bag frozen mixed berries (or your choice; the more tart the better)

1 cup dried banana chips

½ cup powdered buttermilk

½ cup low-fat powdered milk

1 cup cold water per serving

Total weight: 10 ounces
Weight per serving: 1.7 ounces
Total servings: 6 (4 tablespoons per serving)

At home:
Dry berries in a food dehydrator. Once dried, add to banana chips and place both in a food blender. Grind until both become a fine powder. Add powdered buttermilk and powdered milk and store together in a resealable plastic bag.

On the trail:
To make one milk shake, add 4 tablespoons of powder to 1 cup cold water. Mix well.

I found this recipe, and a bag containing its ingredients, in a hiker box in Big Bear City, California, while hiking the Pacific Crest Trail. It can be made into a milk shake or added to your favorite cereal.

MARK MORSE
ANZA, CALIFORNIA

Nutritional information per serving

calories	190
protein	5 g
carbohydrates	22 g
sodium	70 mg
fiber	3 g
fat	10 g
cholesterol	13 mg

Bear Mountain Mocha

Total weight: 13 ounces
Weight per serving: less than 1 ounce
Total servings: 20 (2 tablespoons per serving)

At home:
Mix all dry ingredients together and store in a resealable plastic bag.

On the trail:
Bring 1 cup of water to a boil. Pour water into mug and add 2 tablespoons of mix. Stir well.

We obtained this recipe from the Hughes Family of Tehachapi, California. The name comes from the wonderful mountain on which we used to live in the Tehachapi Range, the southern door to the Sierra Nevada.

TIM AND CHRISTINE CONNERS
CINCINNATI, OHIO

1 cup powdered creamer

1 cup instant coffee

$\frac{1}{2}$ cup sugar

1 single-serving package of milk chocolate instant cocoa mix

$\frac{3}{4}$ teaspoon of cinnamon

1 cup water per serving

Nutritional information per serving

calories	50
protein	0 g
carbohydrates	11 g
sodium	20 mg
fiber	0 g
fat	2 g
cholesterol	0 mg

Pickax Pete's Cowboy Coffee

½ cup coffee grounds

6 cups water

Total weight (without egg): 1 ounce
Total weight (with egg): 3.5 ounces
Weight per serving: less than 1 ounce
Total servings: 6

On the trail:

Over cold water in a pot, float enough coffee grounds to form a skim (thin layer) about ⅛-inch thick. Bring to a boil and remove from the heat. Add a splash of cold water to settle the grounds; or for dramatic effect, use centrifugal force by slinging the pot around your head. (You'd better know what you're doing if you try the latter!) One school says to drink immediately and never reboil coffee grounds. Another keeps adding grounds for the second and third pots, preserving the "mother liquid." Experiment!

Variation: At a Pacific Crest Trail Campfest, Felicia Young gave me her mother's recipe for cowboy coffee. Bring water to a boil, and add coffee mixed with an egg. Yup, the whole thing: white, yolk, and shell. Simmer 12 minutes. Settle grounds with a little cold water. The egg will collect the grounds, so dish it out and discard. Coffee is clear and great!

On the trail, I normally make a pot of coffee every three or four days. North of Steven's Pass on the Pacific Crest Trail one morning, I was joined by Craig and Curtis. As we stopped for breakfast, I offered to share a pot of cowboy coffee. "No, we aren't coffee drinkers," was the reply, "but if you are making a pot. . . ." My son had substituted Starbucks for my generic brand, and the aroma was great. But it was a tactical mistake. From there to Canada, I could hardly get these guys on the trail in the morning without a cup of my cowboy coffee.

Nutritional information per serving

calories	0
protein	0 g
carbohydrates	0 g
sodium	0 mg
fiber	0 g
fat	0 g
cholesterol	0 mg

PETE FISH
"PICKAX PETE"
VENTURA, CALIFORNIA

Sand Canyon Pine Needle Tea

Total weight: 0 ounces
Total servings: 4

½ cup pine needles
1 quart water

On the trail:

In a pot, bring water to a boil. Turn off heat. Add pine needles to the hot water. Cover pot. Let steep for 20 minutes. Then scoop pine needles out with a fork and drink the tea.

GRIFF AND CHRISTINE CORPENING
TEHACHAPI, CALIFORNIA

Authors' note

If you've never had pine tea, you will probably be pleasantly surprised at how good it tastes.

Nutritional information

Very high in vitamin C. Other nutritional information is unavailable.

Vasquez Tea Mix

½ cup Nestea (with sugar)

2 cups powdered Tang

½ cup powdered lemonade mix

1½ cups sugar

1 teaspoon cinnamon

½ teaspoon ground cloves

1 cup water per serving

Total weight: 2 pounds
Weight per serving: less than ½ ounce
Total servings: 70 (1 tablespoon per serving)

At home:
Mix all dry ingredients together. Store in sealed resealable plastic bags. As with most drink mixes, this recipe has a very long shelf life.

On the trail:
To make one serving, bring 1 cup of water to a boil. Add 1 tablespoon of mix to mug and pour in water. Stir well. Can be used to make cold tea as well.

PEG SPRY
AGUA DULCE, CALIFORNIA

Nutritional information per serving

calories	41
protein	0 g
carbohydrates	10 g
sodium	5 mg
fiber	0 g
fat	0 g
cholesterol	0 mg

Sherpa Tea Mix

Total weight: 9 ounces
Weight per serving: less than 1 ounce
Total servings: 12 servings (3 tablespoons per serving)

2 cups low-fat powdered milk

⅓ cup sugar

2 tablespoons Nestea Sweetened Instant Iced Tea Mix with Lemon

1 cup water per serving

At home:
Mix all dry ingredients together and package in a resealable plastic bag.

On the trail:
Bring 1 cup of water to a boil. Add 3 heaping tablespoons of mix to mug and pour in water. Stir well.

ANN MARSHALL
PORT ORCHARD, WASHINGTON

Gauge the fuel consumption of your camp stove against how long it takes to cook your meals, and carry enough fuel plus some for reserves. Keep in mind that high altitudes require more fuel to cook a given amount of food.

JEFFREY HARE
CITRUS HEIGHT, CALIFORNIA

Nutritional information per serving

calories	70
protein	4 g
carbohydrates	13 g
sodium	60 mg
fiber	0 g
fat	0 g
cholesterol	0 mg

Russian Tea Mix

2 cups Tang (or any other orange-flavored drink)

2 cups sweetened instant tea

2 teaspoons cinnamon

1 teaspoon allspice

1 teaspoon ground cloves

Red Hots candies (optional)

1 cup water per serving

Total weight: 1 pound 12 ounces
Weight per serving: less than 1 ounce
Total servings: 32 (2 tablespoons per serving)

At home:

Mix all dry ingredients together and place in resealable plastic bag.

On the trail:

Bring 1 cup of water to a boil. Add 2 tablespoons of mix to mug and pour in water. Stir well. To add a little zing, throw in a few Red Hots.

KATHLEEN CUTSHALL
"THE OLD GRAY GOOSE"
CONNEAUT, OHIO

Nutritional information per serving

calories	90
protein	0 g
carbohydrates	22 g
sodium	0 mg
fiber	0 g
fat	0 g
cholesterol	0 mg

Glacier Ice Slurpy

Total weight: 2.5 ounces
Total servings: 1

½ quart of water

½ cup Kool-Aid (or the powdered fruit drink of your choice)

½ quart of fresh snow

On the trail:

Fill 1-quart water bottle half full with water. Empty powdered drink contents into bottle. Shake well. Add snow to fill the bottle. Shake well. Do not drink too fast, or you may end up with a headache from the ice cold water.

Caution: Untreated water can make you *very* ill. Make sure that the snow you select is clean and pure. If in doubt, don't use it.

KURT THOMPSON
SAN RAMON, CALIFORNIA

Nutritional information per serving

calories	240
protein	0 g
carbohydrates	64 g
sodium	0 mg
fiber	0 g
fat	0 g
cholesterol	0 mg

Ben's Easy Morning Mocha

1 package instant cocoa
mix

1 teaspoon instant coffee

1 teaspoon honey

1 cup water

Total weight: 1 ounce
Total servings: 1

At home:
Package cocoa and coffee together. Carry honey separately.

On the trail:
Bring water to a boil. Add coffee-cocoa mixture along with the honey to mug and pour in water. Stir well.

I use a 3-cup coffeepot on a single-burner propane stove. This makes more than enough water for the instant cocoa-coffee-honey mixture. I use the extra water for my granola or instant oatmeal and to wash the two cups when I'm finished.

BEN YORK
ALPINE, CALIFORNIA

Nutritional information per serving

calories	140
protein	1 g
carbohydrates	28 g
sodium	180 mg
fiber	0 g
fat	3 g
cholesterol	5 mg

Agua Dulce Hot Chocolate

Total weight: 1 pound 2 ounces
Weight per serving: 2.3 ounces
Total servings: 8 (½ cup of mix per serving)

At home:
Mix all dry ingredients together. Store in sealed resealable plastic bag.

On the trail:
To help prevent lumps, add a small amount of cold water to ½ cup of dry mix in mug and stir. Then fill with 1 cup boiling water, stirring well.

PEG SPRY
AGUA DULCE, CALIFORNIA

¼ cup Nestlé's Quik

¼ cup Cremora

2 cups nonfat powdered milk

¼ cup powdered sugar

1 cup water per serving

Nutritional information per serving

calories	220
protein	8 g
carbohydrates	44 g
sodium	140 mg
fiber	0 g
fat	2 g
cholesterol	0 mg

Peaks of Italy Bittersweet Cocoa Mix

3 tablespoons low-fat powdered milk

3 tablespoons Van Houten cocoa powder

3 tablespoons sugar

2¼ cups water

Total weight: 2.5 ounces
Weight per serving: 1.3 ounces
Total servings: 2

At home:
Mix together all dry ingredients and store in a resealable plastic bag.

On the trail:
Pour mix into cold water. Start heating and stir well. Squash all cocoa clumps against the walls of the pot to ensure complete mixing. Serve when sufficiently warm and well mixed.

This was a morning favorite of ours.

Luca de Alfaro
Palo Alto, California

Nutritional information per serving

calories	150
protein	3 g
carbohydrates	33 g
sodium	90 mg
fiber	0 g
fat	1 g
cholesterol	8 mg

Hidden Lake Hot Milk

Total weight: 12 ounces
Weight per serving: 1.2 ounces
Total servings: 10 (2 tablespoons per serving)

2 cups powdered milk

1 tablespoon ground
   cinnamon

½ teaspoon ground
   nutmeg

¼ cup brown sugar

1 cup water per serving

At home:
Mix all dry ingredients together and store in a resealable plastic bag.

On the trail:
Bring 1 cup of water to a boil. Add 2 tablespoons (or more to taste) of mix per mug. To minimize clumping, add a little cold water to the mix first and stir; then fill mugs with boiling water. Stir well.

Because I don't drink coffee, I really appreciate other kinds of hot drinks; and hot milk, especially, is great in the evening. The secret to a smooth beverage is getting the milk dissolved in a little cold water before adding the boiling water.

ANN MARSHALL
PORT ORCHARD, WASHINGTON

Nutritional information per serving

calories	60
protein	5 g
carbohydrates	12 g
sodium	80 mg
fiber	0 g
fat	0 g
cholesterol	0 mg

Burnt Ranch Cinnamon Coffee

1 teaspoon instant coffee

⅛ teaspoon cinnamon (or to taste)

2 teaspoons honey (or to taste)

1 cup water

Total weight: 1 ounce
Total servings: 1

At home:
Mix together coffee and cinnamon and store in a resealable plastic bag. Carry honey separately.

On the trail:
Bring water to a boil. Add coffee-cinnamon mix and the honey to a mug and pour in water. Stir well.

CRAIG SMITH
"SMITTY"
SPRINGFIELD, MISSOURI

Nutritional information per serving

calories	40
protein	0 g
carbohydrates	11 g
sodium	0 mg
fiber	0 g
fat	0 g
cholesterol	0 g

Meal System Examples

Though the name may lead you to believe otherwise, meal systems offer a simple alternative to having to preplan every meal in detail. Using a meal system, you pack a predetermined amount of bulk staples and mix and match to taste once on the trail. This simplifies the initial burden of menu planning, reduces packaging, and increases the flexibility of your meals in the wilderness.

Use the following four examples to help build your own custom system.

Rick Bombaci's Breakfast 101 Hot Cereal System

Pick one item from each of the three categories listed below and combine to make your own unique breakfast cereal. The amount used will vary depending upon what type of cereal you choose as well as your individual appetite.

Category 1: Cereals

Cream of Wheat

Bulgur wheat

Instant oatmeal

Malt-o-Meal

Grits

Granola

Farina

Begin cooking any of the above by adding the appropriate amount of water as well as salt, if desired. Continue by adding any of the following spices or dairy products.

Category 2: Spices

Brown sugar

Nutmeg

Cinnamon

Allspice

Cloves

Powdered or packaged butter

Powdered milk

Be careful with the amount of spices you add. Too much nutmeg, for example, can turn your cereal bitter. Most people wouldn't ordinarily use some of these spices on hot cereal, but you can throw out convention when on the trail.

In addition to the spices, add a handful of one or more varieties of chopped, dried fruit to your hot cereal.

Category 3: Dried Fruit

Apricots

Raisins

Dates

Strawberries

Cranberries

Blueberries

Pineapple

Peaches

Apples

Cherries

Rick provides some final words of wisdom: "Dried fruit is expensive, but hey, you eat whether you're hiking or not. You can also make your own dried fruit, they say, but I've yet to do it myself. And it seems like a big commitment, kind of like marriage."

RICK BOMBACI
ENTERPRISE, OREGON

Authors' note
Rick has hiked over 600 miles of the Appalachian Trail, yet he's afraid to dry his own fruit! Go figure.

Rick Bombaci's Simple Lunch System

Choose a bread product:

Category 1: Bread Product

Bagels

Triscuits

Wheat Thins

English muffin

Top with any of the following:

Category 2: Toppings

Honey

Jam

Butter

Peanut butter

Cheese

Cream cheese

Sausage

Hummus

Mustard

Tahini

Eat with fig bars, trail mix, beef jerky, or fruit leather.

Mustard keeps well on the trail, and tahini, a sesame seed butter, tastes a little bitter but is nevertheless a great alternative to peanut butter.

This meal system is obviously very simple, but an important point is that when you provide yourself a large enough variety of staples, an almost endless variety of combinations results. This is an important virtue to have in your backpack after you've been on the trail for more than a few days.

RICK BOMBACI
ENTERPRISE, OREGON

The Rufners' Lunch System

Dan and Sara Rufner carried common bulk staples when they hiked the entire Pacific Crest Trail, but they nevertheless were able to eat from different menus because they used the philosophy behind meal systems. For lunch, they selected from the following list of foods, usually choosing any three items for lunch, each serving weighing about 4 ounces. Dan would also use peanut butter, honey, and oats as well.

Dried fruit

The Rufners' favorites were mango, pineapple, and papaya but also included fruit rolls, pears, and watermelon. They avoided prepackaged dried fruit because, like many hikers, they experienced intestinal problems that they attributed to the sulfates used in the preservation process.

Chex Mix

They note that this tended to go stale quickly on the trail, however.

Fig Newtons

Energy bars

CliffBar was their favorite brand. They say it was easier to eat than others when cold.

Pretzels

Yogurt pretzels

Granola bar

Mostly used as topping on their pudding.

Animal Crackers

Various trail mixes

Mixed nuts

Primarily macadamia, almonds, and pine nuts as they are high in protein and fats.

Cheese

They would periodically leave their resupply towns carrying a block of cheese.

Pop-Tarts

Dan and Sara Rufner
San Diego, California

Charlie's 624 Dinner System

Charlie Thorpe designed the following system to create a very large variety of meals by mixing and matching four separate categories: dehydrated vegetables, dehydrated meats, carbohydrates, and spices.

Category 1: Dehydrated Vegetables

Use ½ cup of one of the following per meal per person.

English peas

Kidney beans

Lima beans

Black beans

Butter beans

Pinto beans

Green beans

Stir-fry vegetable mix

Broccoli

Corn

Category 2: Dried Meats

Use ¼ cup of one of the following per meal per person.

Canned chicken

Catfish

Lean ground beef

Tuna

Category 3: Carbohydrates

Use ¾ to 1 cup of one of the following per meal per person.

Noodles

Dehydrated hash browns

Rice

Beans

Couscous

Bulgur

Potato flakes

Grits (regular, not instant)

Category 4: Spices

Add your own to taste.

Salt

Pepper

Lemon pepper

Red pepper

Onion powder

Garlic powder

Home-dehydrated salsa

Ground jalapeño

Curry

Italian seasoning

Sage

Bouillon cubes

Small soup-mix packages

Cooking instructions, per person, are simple:

1. Get 3 cups of filtered water and heat.
2. Add ¼ cup of dried meat.
3. Add ½ cup of dehydrated vegetables.
4. Add ¾ to 1 cup of carbohydrates.
5. Add spices to taste.
6. Bring to a boil, then simmer for a couple of minutes.

"Once dehydrated at home, the meat and the vegetables were tossed into the freezer. My wife would pack some into a resupply box every week or two while we were on the trail and mail it to us along with the carbohydrates. Using these various combinations gave us at least 624 different meal possibilities during the trip!"

CHARLIE THORPE
HUNTSVILLE, ALABAMA

Authors' note

Despite their benefits, use meal systems with caution. Ensure that an adequate number of different staples are carried in order to provide a wide range of variety within the system that you select. In addition, before using any meal system for weeks on end, test it at home to make sure that it will work for you. For instance, a meal system may provide a large variety in flavor but not in texture. This may be of no consequence for most people, but for others it will cause them to eventually turn against their food, and you don't want to hate the food you've chosen when you're a month into your border-to-border backpacking trip with five months of meal system resupplies boxed up at home waiting to be shipped to you.

Standard Measurement Conversions

3 teaspoons	1 tablespoon
48 teaspoons	1 cup
2 tablespoons	$\frac{1}{8}$ cup
4 tablespoons	$\frac{1}{4}$ cup
5 tablespoons + 1 teaspoon	$\frac{1}{3}$ cup
8 tablespoons	$\frac{1}{2}$ cup
12 tablespoons	$\frac{3}{4}$ cup
16 tablespoons	1 cup
1 ounce	2 tablespoons
4 ounces	$\frac{1}{2}$ cup
8 ounces	1 cup
$\frac{5}{8}$ cup	$\frac{1}{2}$ cup + 2 tablespoons
$\frac{7}{8}$ cup	$\frac{3}{4}$ cup + 2 tablespoons
2 cups	1 pint
2 pints	1 quart
1 quart	4 cups
1 jigger	$1\frac{1}{2}$ fluid ounces
16 ounces water	1 pound
2 cups fat	1 pound
2 cups or 4 sticks butter	1 pound
2 cups granulated sugar	1 pound
$3\frac{1}{2}$ to 4 cups unsifted powdered sugar	1 pound
$2\frac{1}{4}$ cups packed brown sugar	1 pound
4 cups sifted flour	1 pound
$3\frac{1}{2}$ cups unsifted whole-wheat flour	1 pound
8 to 10 egg whites	1 cup
12 to 14 egg yolks	1 cup
1 whole lemon, squeezed	3 tablespoons juice
1 whole orange, squeezed	$\frac{1}{3}$ cup juice

Drying Conversions

The following weights and measures may vary slightly due to a variety of factors, including brand selection, depth of cut, dehydrating method, and equipment.

Undried Item	Dried Volume	Dried Weight
1 tablespoon fresh herbs	1 teaspoon	less than 1 ounce
1 tablespoon mustard	1 teaspoon	less than 1 ounce
1 garlic clove, pressed	$\frac{1}{8}$ teaspoon powder	less than 1 ounce
1 pound frozen peas	1 cup	4 ounces
1 pound carrots, cooked and sliced	$\frac{1}{2}$ cup	2 ounces
1 pound potatoes, boiled and sliced	$1\frac{1}{2}$ cups	4 ounces
1 pound diced onions	1 cup	1 ounce
1 pound frozen French sliced green beans	2 cups	$1\frac{1}{2}$ ounces
1 pound diced celery	$\frac{1}{3}$ cup	$\frac{1}{2}$ ounce
1 pound fresh mushrooms, sliced	$2\frac{1}{2}$ cups	1 ounce
1 pound fresh green bell pepper	$\frac{3}{4}$ cup	$1\frac{1}{2}$ ounces
1 pound fresh jalapeño peppers	$1\frac{1}{3}$ cups	1 ounce
1 pound frozen mixed vegetables	$\frac{3}{4}$ cup	$3\frac{1}{2}$ ounces
1 (15-ounce) can mixed vegetables	$\frac{1}{2}$ cup	$1\frac{1}{2}$ ounces
1 (6-ounce) can medium diced olives	$\frac{1}{2}$ cup	1 ounce
1 (15-ounce) can pinto beans	1 cup	$2\frac{1}{2}$ ounces
1 (15-ounce) can black beans	$1\frac{1}{4}$ cups	$3\frac{1}{2}$ ounces
1 (15-ounce) can kidney beans	1 cup	$2\frac{1}{2}$ ounces
1 pound steamed, chopped zucchini	$\frac{1}{3}$ cup	$\frac{1}{2}$ ounce
1 pound frozen sliced broccoli	1 cup	1 ounce
1 pound sliced Roma tomatoes	1 cup	1 ounce
1 (6-ounce) can tomato paste	Leather roll	$1\frac{1}{2}$ ounces
1 pound salsa	$\frac{1}{2}$ cup	$\frac{1}{2}$ ounce
1 pound sliced apples	$1\frac{1}{2}$ cups	3 ounces
1 pound sliced bananas	$1\frac{1}{2}$ cups	4 ounces
1 (20-ounce) can diced pineapple	$\frac{3}{4}$ cup	2 ounces
1 pound trimmed watermelon	1 cup	1 ounce
1 pound frozen cherries	$\frac{1}{2}$ cup	2 ounces
1 pound sliced turkey breast	$1\frac{1}{2}$ cups	6 ounces
1 pound ground beef (gravel)	1 cup	5 ounces
1 pound or 3 breasts poached chicken	2 cups	4 ounces
1 (5-ounce) can chunk light chicken	$\frac{1}{2}$ cup	$1\frac{1}{2}$ ounces
1 (6-ounce) can pink salmon	$\frac{1}{2}$ cup	$1\frac{1}{2}$ ounces
1 (6-ounce) can water-packed tuna	$\frac{1}{2}$ cup	$1\frac{1}{2}$ ounces
1 cup whole milk	$\frac{1}{2}$ cup powdered	2 ounces

National Scenic and Historic Trails

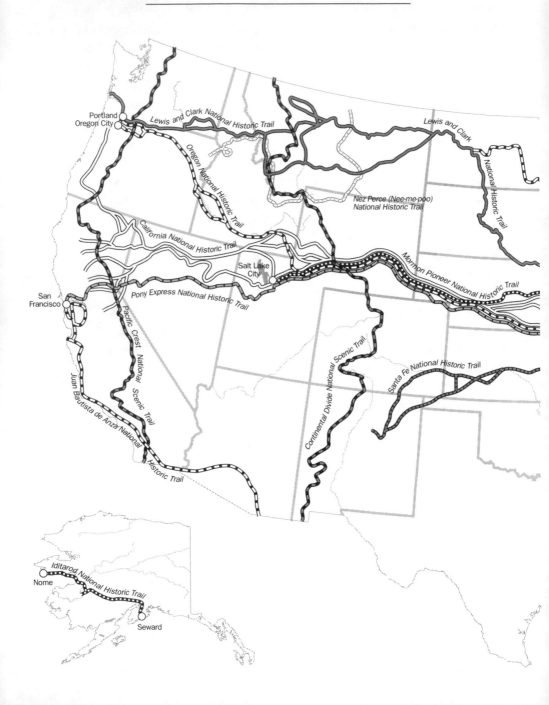

North Country National Scenic Trail

Ice Age National Scenic Trail

Council Bluffs

St. Joseph

Kansas City

St. Louis

Trail Of Tears National Historic Trail

National

Scenic Trail

Appalachian

Washington, D.C.

Potomac Heritage National Scenic Trail

Overmountain Victory National Historic Trail

Natchez Trace National Scenic Trail

Selma to Montgomery National Historic Trail

Selma   Montgomery

Florida National Scenic Trail

National Scenic and Historic Trails

What follows is a brief description of all of the federally established National Scenic and Historic Trails of the United States. The longest trail comprises almost 6,000 miles, and the shortest covers 34 miles. The majority of the trails are at least 1,000 miles in length. The National Scenic Trails emphasize the natural beauty of the areas they traverse, with the primary goal being to maximize the user's appreciation of the land. The National Historic Trails place emphasis on a specific segment of American history and, in spanning hundreds or thousands of miles, are designed to enlarge the trail user's exposure to the events surrounding that particular era in time.

Many of the trails listed below are currently under construction along portions of their length, with intervening gaps where no tread exists for many miles. Some of the trails have been completed from end to end, stretching thousands of miles in an unbroken ribbon. This is the case with the Appalachian and the Pacific Crest trails. Some of the trails follow paved roadways for much of their length, either by design or because the planned tread has not yet been built, and some require cross-country navigational skills in the absence of trail tread. More information on each of the trails is available through the contact information listed below each trail description or by going to the National Park Service website at www.nps.gov.

It is a painstaking, costly, and time-consuming process to build trail tread, with private property easement issues often the largest and costliest hurdle in the construction of a trail. Volunteer trail associations help preserve and protect the portions of a trail that have already been built and also work toward the completion of the entire trail as originally envisioned. There is probably a long trail near where you live that could use your support. We encourage you to contact one of the trail associations found in the list below for more information.

There are enough hiking opportunities in this list to satisfy a lifetime of trail trekking, but even this is not a complete list of all long-distance trails. Hundreds of additional trails can be found throughout the United States offering the hiker and equestrian many more miles of adventure. A trail user can even link together thousands of miles of relatively short, unnamed trails, especially in the mountains of the Rockies, Cascades and Sierra Nevada, providing endless long-distance trekking potential. If you haven't yet discovered the magic of long-distance trails, we hope that this list will help you do so.

Appalachian National Scenic Trail
Established in 1968
2,155 miles

The Appalachian National Scenic Trail is a footpath spanning the Appalachian Mountain ridge line. Benton MacKay first envisioned the trail in 1921 as a continuous greenbelt from Maine to Georgia. This trail was developed with the help of volunteer hiking clubs and is maintained today by several nonprofit groups, the largest of which is the Appalachian Trail Conference with thirty-two affiliated volunteer trail clubs. The trail is a unit of the National Parks System, and ninety-seven percent of the trail is protected by federal or state ownership. The trail passes through the following fourteen states:

Maine, New Hampshire, Vermont, Massachusetts, Connecticut, New York, New Jersey, Pennsylvania, Maryland, West Virginia, Virginia, Tennessee, North Carolina, and Georgia. There are shelters spaced along the trail for covered overnight camping. This "grandfather" of the National Scenic Trails sees an average of 175 people travel the entire trail each year, with many thousands more hiking smaller segments.

Appalachian Trail Conference
P.O. Box 807
Harpers Ferry, WV 25425
(304) 535-6068
(304) 535-2667 Fax
E-mail: info@atconf.org
www.atconf.org/

National Park Service
Appalachian National Scenic Trail Office
Harpers Ferry Center
Harpers Ferry, WV 25425
(304) 535-6278
(304) 535-6270 Fax
E-mail: appa@nps.gov
www.nps.gov/aptr

California National Historic Trail
Established in 1992
5,665 miles

The 1849 gold rush began with the discovery of gold at Sutter's Mill in California. Starting at seven different points along the Missouri River, gold seekers followed the Great Platte River Road, overlapping with Oregon and Mormon emigrants' trails, until they had crossed the crest of the Rocky Mountains. From there they chose a route through the Sierra Nevada. The course they followed was dependent upon the availability of water and forage, the condition of their livestock and wagons, the knowledge of their guides, and the presence of Indians. The California Trail carried the greatest mass migration in American history. More than 200,000 gold seekers and farmers made their way to California during the 1840s and 1850s. Today, more than 1,000 miles of trail ruts can still be seen between Casper, Wyoming, and the coast of California. The trail passes through the states of Missouri, Kansas, Nebraska, Colorado, Wyoming, Idaho, Utah, Nevada, and Oregon, before crossing California.

Oregon-California Trails Association
P.O. Box 1019
Independence, MO 64051-0519
(816) 252-2276
(816) 836-0989 Fax
www.calcite.rocky.edu/octa/

National Park Service
Long Distance Trails Office
324 S. State Street
P.O. Box 45155
Salt Lake City, UT 84145-0155
(801) 539-4095
(801) 539-4098 Fax
www.nps.gov/cali/

Continental Divide National Scenic Trail
Established in 1978
3,200 miles

When completed, the Continental Divide Trail will extend from Mexico to Canada along the crest of the Rocky Mountains. At present, only 795 miles have been officially completed in a section that runs from the Canadian border, through Montana and Idaho, and on into Yellowstone National Park. Smaller segments have recently opened in other states as well. This trail passes through some of our nation's most beautiful scenic areas, including Glacier National Park, ten national forests, wilderness areas such as the Bob Marshall and Anaconda Pintler, and several state and Bureau of Land Management resource areas. Elevations along the trail through Montana and Idaho range from 4,200 feet to nearly 10,000 feet in the Bitterroot Range. More than ninety percent of the trail is within 5 miles of the Continental Divide, and much of it is on the divide itself. This trail is open to hikers, pack and saddle animals, and, in some locations, off-road motorized vehicles. It is considered by some to be the most rugged of all the long-distance trails.

Continental Divide Trail Alliance
P.O. Box 628
Pine, CO 80470
(303) 838-3760
(303) 838-3960 Fax
E-mail: CDNST@aol.com
www.CDTrail.org

Continental Divide Trail Society
3704 N. Charles St., #601
Balto, MD 21218-2300
(410) 235-9610
E-mail: cdtsociety@aol.com
www.gorp.com/cdts/

U.S.D.A. Forest Service
Northern Regional Office (Region 1)
Federal Building
P.O. Box 7669
Missoula, MT 59807-7669
(406) 329-3150
(406) 329-3132 Fax
www.fs.fed.us/intro/directory/rg-1.htm

U.S.D.A. Forest Service
Rocky Mountain Regional Office (Region 2)
740 Simms
Golden, CO 80401
(303) 275-5045
(303) 275-5366 Fax
www.fs.fed.us/intro/directory/rg-2.htm

U.S.D.A. Forest Service
Southwestern Region (Region 3)
Federal Building
517 Gold Avenue, SW
Albuquerque, NM 87102
(505) 842-3236
(505) 842-3800 Fax
www.fs.fed.us/intro/directory/rg-3.htm

U.S.D.A. Forest Service
Intermountain Regional Office (Region 4)
1594 W. N. Temple, #3310
Box 144600
Salt Lake City, UT 84114-4600
(801) 538-5358
(801) 533-4111 Fax
www.fs.fed.us/intro/directory/rg-4.htm

Florida National Scenic Trail
Established in 1983
1,300 Miles

The Florida Trail was designated as a National Scenic Trail in 1986. When complete, the trail will extend from Big Cypress National Preserve in south Florida, through Florida's three national forests, to Gulf Islands National Seashore in the western panhandle. This trail is enjoyed especially in the winter as it passes through the only subtropical landscape in the United States. There are many side loop trails that connect to nearby historic sites and other places of interest. More than 1,000 miles have been completed to date, with about 300 miles officially open for public use.

Florida Trail Association
P.O. Box 13708
Gainesville, FL 32604-1708
(800) 343-1882
(352) 378-8823 Fax
E-mail: fta@florida-trail.org
www.florida-trail.org/

U.S.D.A. Forest Service
National Forests in Florida
325 John Knox Road, #F-100
Tallahassee, Florida, 32303
(850) 942-9376
(850) 942-9305 Fax
www.fs.fed.us/intro/directory/rg-8.htm

Ice Age National Scenic Trail
Established in 1980
1,000 miles

Following the Ice Age, the glaciers retreated from North America and left behind a long
chain of moraine hills. Ray Zillmer conceived of a trail along these hills, and today, with
the help of the State of Wisconsin and the Ice Age Park and Trail Foundation, almost half
the trail is now open for public use. The trail generally follows the end moraines of the
most recent glaciation, although it diverges from them at times to pass by other features
of the glacial landscape and to allow trekkers to catch a glimpse of the Driftless Area. This
trail passes through the most remote sections of Wisconsin.

Ice Age Park and Trail Foundation, Inc.
207 E. Buffalo Street, #515
Milwaukee, WI 53202-5712
(414) 278-8518
(414) 278-8665 Fax
E-mail: iat@exec.pc.com
www.iceagetrail.org

National Park Service
Ice Age National Scenic Trail
700 Rayovac Drive, Suite 100
Madison, WI 53711
(608) 264-5610
(608) 264-5615 Fax
www.nps.gov/iatr

Iditarod National Historic Trail
Established in 1978
2,450 miles total
900 miles main route

The Iditarod National Historic Trail is made up of a network of more than 2,400 miles of trails once used by ancient hunters and, later, by early twentieth-century gold seekers and their dog teams. The trail obtained its name from a nineteenth-century Athabascan Indian village on the Iditarod River near the site of a 1908 gold discovery. It begins at Seward, Alaska, and ends at Nome, Alaska. Most of the trail is usable only during Alaska's winter season when the rivers and tundra are frozen. Today, the annual 1,150-mile Iditarod Sled Dog Race follows the trail from Anchorage to Nome. Other activities that take place on the trail include the 210-mile Iditasport Race for skiers, mountain bikers, and snowshoers, as well as the Alaska Gold Rush Classic Snowmachine Race.

Iditarod Trail Blazers
P.O. Box 1923
Seward, AK 99644

Iditarod Trail Blazers
Knik Chapter
H230 Box 5460
Wasilla, AK 99694
(907) 376-5562

Iditarod Trail Committee
P.O. Box 870800
Wasilla, AK 99687
(907) 376-5155

Bureau of Land Management
Anchorage District
6881 Abbott Loop Road
Anchorage, AK 99507
(907) 267-1207
(907) 267-1267 Fax
www.ak.blm.gov/ado/inhthome.html

Juan Bautista de Anza National Historic Trail
Established in 1990
1,200 miles

This trail commemorates the travels made by a party of Spanish colonists led by Colonel Juan Bautista de Anza, who set out from Mexico in 1775 to establish an overland route to California. The colonists' goal was to build a presidio and mission overlooking what is now the Golden Gate area of San Francisco and to secure it from British and Russian threat. The party of thirty families, a dozen soldiers, and numerous livestock made their way through the deserts of Arizona and Southern California, taking six months to reach their destination. This trail attempts to follow their original route.

Amigos de Anza
1350 Castle Rock Road
Walnut Canyon, CA 94598
(510) 926-1081
E-mail: htrails@earthlink.net
www.therapure.com/anza-trail/

Anza Trail Coalition of Arizona
P.O. Box 42612
Tucson, AZ 85733-2612
(520) 325-0909

National Park Service
Pacific-Great Basin Office
Planning Partnership Team
600 Harrison St., Suite 600
San Francisco, CA 94107-1372
(415) 427-1438
(415) 744-4043 Fax
www.nps.gov/juba/

Lewis and Clark National Historic Trail
Established in 1978
3,700 miles

In 1804, Meriwether Lewis and William Clark were commissioned by President Thomas Jefferson to explore the newly acquired Louisiana Territory and what was known as the Oregon Country. The expedition began by boat from what is today called Wood River, Illinois, and followed the Missouri River upstream. By 1805 the party reached the Pacific Ocean at the mouth of the Columbia River, returning east the following year. The Lewis and Clark National Historic Trail begins in Missouri and passes through Iowa, Kansas, Nebraska, South Dakota, North Dakota, Montana, Idaho, Washington, and Oregon.

Lewis and Clark Trail Heritage Foundation, Inc.
P.O. Box 3434
Great Falls, MT 59403
(406) 454-1234
(406) 454-0448 Fax
www.lewisandclark.org

National Lewis and Clark Bicentennial Council
1101 Officers Road
U.S. Grant House
Vancouver, WA 98661
(888) 999-1803
(503) 234-1794 Fax
E-mail: bicentennial@lewisandclark200.org
www.lewisandclark200.org
www.lewis-clark.org

National Park Service
Lewis and Clark National Historic Trail
700 Rayovac Drive, Suite 100
Madison, WI 53711
(608) 264-5610
(608) 264-5615 Fax
www.nps.gov/lecl/

Mormon Pioneer National Historic Trail
Established in 1978
1,300 miles

From 1846 to 1869, more than 70,000 Mormons traveled west to seek refuge from religious persecution. They primarily used a trail connecting the Midwest with the western territories that had been previously established by American Indians, European trappers, missionaries, soldiers, teamsters, stagecoach drivers, Pony Express riders, and overland emigrants. The Mormons began their westward trek from Nauvoo, Illinois, and ended their journey in an area near the Great Salt Lake that later became part of the Utah Territory and finally the State of Utah.

Mormon Trails Association
300 S. Rio Grande
Salt Lake City, Utah 84101
(801) 544-1579
E-mail: gtelison@sisna.com

National Park Service
Long-Distance Trails Office, SLC
324 S. State Street
P.O. Box 45155
Salt Lake City, UT 84145-0155
(801) 539-4095
(801) 539-4098 Fax
www.nps.gov/mopi/

Natchez Trace National Scenic Trail
Established in 1983
450 miles

The Natchez Trace National Scenic Trail lies within the Natchez Trace Parkway greenbelt and extends for 450 miles from Natchez, Mississippi, to Nashville, Tennessee. The trace began as a series of animal tracks used by Native American hunters including the Natchez, Chickasaw, and Choctaw tribes. As early as 1733, French maps depict an Indian trail running from Natchez toward the northeast. The trail was later used by early explorers, Kaintuck boatmen, post riders, and the military, including General Andrew Jackson after his victory at the Battle of New Orleans. Improvements to the route were made, and by 1810, the trace was a heavily traveled wilderness road. Since the 1930s, the National Park Service has been constructing a modern parkway that closely follows the course of the original trace. Today, almost 90 percent of the parkway is complete.

Natchez Trace Trail Conference, Inc.
P.O. Box 1236
Jackson, MS 39215-1236
(601) 956-0045
E-mail: jhodonttc@aol.com

National Park Service
Superintendent, Natchez Trace Parkway
2680 Natchez Trace Parkway
Tupelo, MS 38801
(601) 680-4014
(601) 680-4034 Fax
www.nps.gov/natt
www.gorp.com/gorp/resource/us_trail/natchez.htm
www.public.iastate.edu/~sfr/nts/ntnst.html

Nez Perce National Historic Trail
Established in 1986
1,170 miles

This trail begins in Oregon and passes through Idaho, Montana, and Wyoming. The trail commemorates the journey of the Nez Perce Indians who were forced from their ancestral homelands in 1877 and relocated to a reservation east of Lewiston, Idaho. During this journey, conflict erupted between settlers and the Nez Perce. The U.S. Army was called to intercede. Hoping to find refuge in Canada, the resisting band headed east across the Rocky Mountains, through the newly established Yellowstone National Park, and into the Great Plains. This journey ended only 40 miles from the Canadian border, where the band was overtaken by the army at the Battle of the Bear Paw in Northern Montana.

Nez Perce National Historic Trail Foundation
P.O. Box 20197
Missoula, MT 59801
(208) 843-2253
www.public.iastate.edu/~sfr/npnhtf.html

U.S.D.A. Forest Service
Northern Regional Office (Region 1)
Federal Building
P.O. Box 7669
Missoula, MT 59807
(406) 329-3602
(406) 329-3132 Fax
www.fs.fed.us/intro/directory/rg-1.htm

Nez Perce National Historical Park
Route1, P.O. Box 100
Highway 95
Spalding, ID 83540
(208) 843-2261
(208) 843-2124 Fax
www.nps.gov/nepe/

North Country National Scenic Trail
Established in 1980
3,200 miles

The North Country Trail links New York's Adirondack Mountains with the Missouri River in North Dakota. More than 1,400 miles of the trail are complete and pass through a vast variety of environments in the northeastern and north central United States. Beginning in New York, the trail meanders westward among the hardwood forests of Pennsylvania, through the countryside of Ohio and southern Michigan, along the shores of the Great Lakes, through the glacier-carved forests, lakes, and streams of northern Wisconsin and Minnesota, and terminates in the plains of North Dakota.

North Country Trail Association
49 Monroe Center, NW, #200B
Grand Rapids, MI 49503
(616) 454-5506
(616) 454-7139 Fax
E-mail: NCTAssoc@aol.com

Finger Lakes Trail Conference, Inc.
P.O. Box 18048
Rochester, NY 14618-0048
(716) 288-7191
www.fingerlakes.net/trailsystem

Buckeye Trail Association
P.O. Box 254
Worthington, OH 43085
(419) 447-5464
E-mail: info@buckeyetrail.org
www.ne-ohio.net/bta/

National Park Service
North Country National Scenic Trail
700 Rayovac Drive, Suite 100
Madison, WI 53711
(608) 264-5610
(608) 264-5615 Fax
E-mail: Bill_Menke@nps.gov
www.nps.gov/noco

Oregon National Historic Trail
Established in 1978
2,170 miles

The Oregon Trail was once the pathway to the Pacific for gold seekers, missionaries, fur traders, and emigrants. Beginning in 1841, and for the following twenty years, an estimated 400,000 people traveled from the Missouri River to Oregon's Willamette River. Today, the trail begins in Missouri and passes through Kansas, Nebraska, Wyoming, Idaho, and Oregon. One can still find more than 300 miles of discernible wagon ruts as well as 125 historic sites along the trail.

Oregon-California Trails Association
P.O. Box 1019
Independence, MO 64051-0519
(816) 252-2276
(816) 836-0989 Fax
www.calcite.rocky.edu/octa/
members.aol.com/octanw/maps/clickable.html

National Park Service
Long Distance Trails Office, SLC
324 S. State Street
P.O. Box 45155
Salt Lake City, UT 84145-0155
(801) 539-4095
(801) 539-4098 Fax
www.nps.gov/oreg/

Overmountain Victory National Historic Trail
Established in 1980
300 miles

In 1780, during the Revolutionary War, patriots from Virginia, Tennessee, and North Carolina formed a militia to drive British troops out of the southern colonies. This trail marks their fourteen-day trek across the Appalachians to the Piedmont region of the Carolinas. The defeat of British troops at the Battle of King's Mountain was a major turning point in the war, setting in motion events that eventually led to the British surrender. Each year, this historic event is reenacted by many folks following the original march to King's Mountain. Today much of the trail has become road; only a small 20-mile portion remains a foot trail.

Overmountain Victory Trail Association
Sycamore Shoals State Historic Area
1651 West Elk Avenue
Elizabethton, TN 37643
(615) 543-5808

National Park Service
Southeast Regional Office
Atlanta Federal Center, 1924 Building
100 Alabama Street, SW
Atlanta, GA 30303
(404) 562-3124
(404) 562-3267 Fax
www.nps.gov/ovvi

Pacific Crest National Scenic Trail
Established in 1968
2,638 miles

The Pacific Crest Trail stretches from Mexico to Canada, following the mountain crests of the ranges of southern California, the Sierra Nevada, and the Cascade Mountains of California, Oregon, and Washington. In 1968, the Pacific Crest Trail, along with the Appalachian Trail, were established by Congress as the first of the federally protected National Scenic Trails. The Pacific Crest Trail is a wildland route, open only to hikers and equestrians, and is notable in that the entire trail is complete. Trail construction began in 1928, integrating and linking several of the West's most famous trails, including the John Muir Trail. The Pacific Crest Trail was officially completed in 1993 and passes through twenty-four national forests, seven national parks, one national recreation area, one national monument, thirty-three wilderness areas, six state/provincial parks, and four areas administered by the Bureau of Land Management.

Pacific Crest Trail Association
5325 Elkhorn Boulevard, #256
Sacramento, CA 95842
(888) 728-7245
(916) 349-2109
(916) 349-1268 Fax
E-mail: info@pcta.org
www.pcta.org

U.S.D.A. Forest Service
Pacific Southwest Regional Office (Region 5)
2245 Morello Avenue
Pleasant Hill, CA 94523
(510) 609-6175
(510) 687-0125 Fax
www.fs.fed.us/intro/directory/rg-5.htm

U.S.D.A. Forest Service
Pacific Northwest Regional Office (Region 6)
333 S.W. First Avenue
P.O. Box 3623
Portland, Oregon 97208-3623
(503) 808-2443
(503) 808-2429 Fax
www.fs.fed.us/intro/directory/rg-6.htm

Pony Express National Historic Trail
Established in 1992
1,855 miles

This trail follows the route once used by the Pony Express, which began in 1860 as a vital mail route connecting the eastern United States to California and passing through the states of Missouri, Kansas, Nebraska, Colorado, Wyoming, Utah, Nevada, and California. Dozens of riders and horses carried more than 35,000 pieces of mail through the deserts, plains, and mountains around the clock to see the mail delivered. The average travel time from St. Joseph, Missouri, to Sacramento, California, was only ten days on horseback.

National Pony Express Association
528 12th Road
Oketo, KS 66518-8644
(913) 744-3333
E-mail: xptom@ccnet.com
www.ccnet.com/~xptom/

Pony Express Trails Association
139 San Antonio Way
Sacramento, CA 95819

National Park Service
Long Distance Trails Office, SLC
324 S. State Street
P.O. Box 45155
Salt Lake City, UT 84145-0155
(801) 539-4095
(801) 539-4098 Fax
www.nps.gov/poex

Potomac Heritage National Scenic Trail
Established in 1983
704 miles

This trail commemorates both the history and recreational uses of the Potomac River. This trail is not yet complete; however, three components have been officially opened to date. These include a 184-mile long Chesapeake & Ohio Canal towpath from Georgetown, in Washington, D.C., to Cumberland, Maryland; the 17-mile Mount Vernon Trail, connecting Washington, D.C., and Mount Vernon, Virginia; and the 75-mile Laurel Highlands National Recreation Trail in Pennsylvania.

Potomac Heritage Partnership
1623 28th Street, NW
Washington, D.C. 20007
(202) 338-1118
(202) 333-2887 Fax
E-mail: php1623@aol.com

Allegheny Trail Alliance
P.O. Box 186
Latrobe, PA 15650
(724) 537-6900
(724) 537-6906 Fax
(800) ATA-BIKE

National Park Service
Potomac Valley Field Office
P.O. Box B
Harpers Ferry, WV 25425
(304) 535-4014
(304) 737-5275 Fax
www.nps.gov/pohe/

Santa Fe National Historic Trail
Established in 1987
1,203 miles

The Santa Fe Trail was created in 1821. It was developed by U.S. and Mexican traders following American Indian travel routes. At the time, New Mexico belonged to Mexico, and the trail became a commercial link between Mexico and the United States. The trail was also used by the U.S. Army during the Mexican and Civil Wars. The Santa Fe Trail originates in New Franklin, Missouri, and passes through Kansas and Colorado before terminating in Santa Fe, New Mexico. More than 200 miles of wagon ruts remain visible along the trail.

Santa Fe Trail Association
Santa Fe Trail Center
Route 3
Larned, KS 67550
(316) 285-2054
www.nmhu.edu/research/sftrail/sfta.htm

National Park Service
Long Distance Trails Group Office—Santa Fe
P.O. Box 728
Santa Fe, NM 87504-0728
(505) 988-6888
(505) 986-5214 Fax
E-mail: lodi_administration@nps.gov
www.nps.gov/safe/

Selma-to-Montgomery National Historic Trail
Established in 1996
54 miles

The Selma-to-Montgomery Trail recognizes the three marches made by protesters of the discriminatory practices that prevented African-Americans from voting in the Deep South. As the name suggests, the trail begins in Selma, Alabama, and follows roadway to Montgomery, Alabama. The first march took place on Sunday, March 7, 1965. Upon reaching the Edmund Pettus Bridge, the marchers were brutally attacked by law enforcement officers. The second march began on March 9, but the participants were again turned away at the bridge. The third and final march began on March 21 and reached Montgomery successfully on March 26, in part due to the assistance of National Guardsmen. This trek, and the publicity it received, strengthened the nation's determination to enact strong voting rights legislation that led to the passage of the Voting Rights Act of 1965.

Tuskegee Institute National Historic Site
1212 Old Montgomery Road
Tuskegee Institute, AL 36088
(334) 727-6390
(334) 727-4597 Fax

National Park Service
Atlanta Federal Center
1924 Building
100 Alabama St. SW
Atlanta, GA 30303
(888) 333-1791
(404) 562-3175
www.cr.nps.gov/nr/travel/civilrights/al4.htm

Trail of Tears National Historic Trail
Established in 1987
2,052 miles

In the late 1830s, pressure from settlers and the U.S. Army forced 16,000 Cherokee Indians from their homelands in the southeastern states to lands west of the Mississippi River. Thousands died along the way. Although different routes were taken to the Oklahoma Territory, the designated trail today follows two of the principal routes: a water trail (1,226 miles) along the Tennessee, Ohio, Mississippi, and Arkansas Rivers and an overland route (826 miles) from Chattanooga, Tennessee, to Tahlequah, Oklahoma.

Trail of Tears Association
American Indian Center of Arkansas
1100 N. University, #133
Little Rock, AR 72207
(501) 666-9032
(501) 666-5875 Fax

National Park Service
Long Distance Trails Group Office—Santa Fe
P.O. Box 728
Santa Fe, NM 87504-0728
(505) 988-6888
(505) 986-5214 Fax

About Our Contributors

Ed Acheson
Cincinnati, Ohio

Ed is an intellectual property attorney. In 1981, he hiked the Pacific Crest Trail from the Mexican border northward to Interstate 80 in northern California. Since then, he has continued hiking the Pacific Crest Trail in sections and has reached Drakesbad, California. He has recently traveled the Boundary Waters Canoe Area Wilderness of Minnesota as well as Quetico Park in Canada. He is currently planning a trip to the top of Denali Peak in Alaska.

Gary Adams
"Doctari"
Cincinnati, Ohio

Gary works as a paramedic for a local hospital to pay his hiking bills. He is currently section-hiking the Appalachian Trail northward and has reached Deep Gap in North Carolina. When he was eight years old, he fell in love at first sight with the Appalachian Trail. Thirty-five years later, he is finally realizing his dream to hike the entire trail. Gary is married and has two children.

Chuck and Susan Atkinson
Dorris, California

Chuck and Susan have the goal of walking the Pacific Crest Trail section by section from Castle Crags, California, northward to the Canadian border. They have completed almost the entire stretch to Crater Lake, Oregon. They repeatedly hike their favorite sections of the trail.

Emmett Autrey
"Ol Kooger"
Amarillo, Texas

Emmett began backpacking the Pacific Crest Trail in sections, starting at the Mexican border in June 1992. He has made nine trips, totaling over 500 miles to date. His goal is to reach the Canadian border by the year 2006. His trail name comes from his attitude about unnecessary ascents: "Why go over if you can go around?" Just like an old cougar with a broken tooth! Emmett is married and has three grown sons and three granddaughters. He is a water production superintendent for the city of Amarillo.

Bob and Laurel Ballou
Sacramento, California

Bob is the executive director of the Pacific Crest Trail Association. He formerly served on the executive staff of the Boy Scouts of America. Laurel works for REI in Sacramento. Laurel and Bob began backpacking in 1978 when they took their two young boys on their first family trek in the backcountry of Yosemite. They continued their annual family outings until the boys left home. Now the couple continues on their own, covering much of the Central Sierra region.

Rick Bombaci
Enterprise, Oregon

Rick completed 600 miles of the Appalachian Trail in 1993, beginning on Mount Katahdin in Maine and ending at Cheshire, Massachusetts. He hopes to hike the Pacific Crest Trail in the near future.

Dan and Tina Breedlove
"The Honeymooners"
Eudora, Kansas

Beginning at the Mexican border, Dan and Tina hiked the Pacific Crest Trail with their two dogs, Kymba and Elli, in 1995. Tina made it as far north as South Lake Tahoe in northern California while Dan continued his journey to Canada via the Pacific Crest bike route. Dan is in law school and Tina is working toward a Master's in Psychology. They have one child.

Deborah Brill
Scott "Marty" Place
Berkeley, California

Marty thru-hiked the Appalachian Trail in 1992 and the Pacific Crest Trail in 1996. He loves rock climbing, canoeing, whitewater kayaking, and mountaineering. Deborah has backpacked extensively in Alaska, Nepal, and throughout the United States. Deborah thru-hiked the Pacific Crest Trail in 1996. She has a passion for and experience in leading outdoor trips for at-risk youth. Like Marty, she enjoys rock climbing, whitewater kayaking, canoeing, and mountaineering.

Ursula Brower
South Lake Tahoe, California

Ursula completed the entire Pacific Crest Trail with her husband in 1979. "We were founding members of the Pacific Crest Trail Conference (now the Pacific Crest Trail Association) when it was directed by Warren Rogers." Ursula is a registered nurse in a maternity ward, and her husband is a firefighter for the U.S.D.A. Forest Service. They assist many hikers each year who pass through the Lake Tahoe area. She says, "You can always spot the Pacific Crest Trailers along the road. They have a certain look about them!"

Sandy Lee Burns
Prospect, Oregon

Sandy is a Pacific Crest Trail Association member who has completed the Washington section of the Pacific Crest Trail three times, the Oregon section once, and sections in northern California. She has also hiked the John Muir Trail once. She hikes with her llama, Dancing Cloud. She also performs trail maintenance in Crater Lake National Park in Oregon.

Kevin Corcoran
Palmdale, California

Kevin has been hiking and backpacking since he was a Boy Scout in Hygiene, Colorado, nearly twenty years ago. He enjoys hiking the desert, especially the canyons of Arizona, but also climbing an occasional fourteener. He has hiked many local sections of the neighboring Pacific Crest Trail in the San Gabriel Mountains.

Griff and Christine Corpening
Tehachapi, California

Griff and Christine own and manage the Tehachapi Tea Company, where Christine produces health-oriented tea blends. Griff is also an engineer at NASA's Dryden Flight Research Center. The Corpenings have extensive outdoor experience and, in their spare time, operate an outdoor wilderness skills school. They have one son, Jack.

Pam Coz-Hill
Visalia, California

Pam is a regular on the Pacific Crest Trail. She is the owner and manager of Mike's Quality Cameras in Visalia. She is a nature photographer and also hikes in northern Arizona and southern Utah.

Kathleen A. Cutshall
"The Old Gray Goose"
Conneaut, Ohio

Kathleen was fifty-three years old when she first attempted a backpacking trip on the Appalachian Trail. She has been married for more than forty years and has three children and ten grandchildren as well as a large number of assorted pets. She has since returned to Vermont and completed hiking the Long Trail. She has also ventured to Glacier National Park with her friends and hiked the Nyack-Coal Creek Wilderness Area Loop Trail. Kathleen loves to cook, and she assisted in the testing of the recipes for this book.

Cathy Czachorowski
Torrington, Connecticut

Cathy completed 2,065 miles of the Pacific Crest Trail in 1996, traveling from the Mexican border to Olallie Lake, Oregon. She returned to complete the trail northward to Canada in 1997. She works as a veterinary assistant.

Walt and Jane Daniels
Mohegan Lake, New York

Walt and Jane have been hiking the Appalachian Trail in sections. They have completed most of the trail through New York and Maine. Both are 1997 New York Vibram Volunteer of the Year recipients. Jane is on the boards of the Appalachian Trail Conference and the New York-New Jersey Trail Conference. Walt is a trail supervisor on the Appalachian Trail. They are long-time gourmet camp cooks and believe that "if you can cook it at home, you can cook an adaptation of it on the trail."

Mark Davis
"Crawls with Bears"
San Francisco, California

Mark hiked more than 400 miles of the Pacific Crest Trail in 1996 before he came upon and joined a Pacific Crest Trail Association work crew because they had better food than he had in his pack. Mark teaches English at Sacred Heart Preparatory School in Atherton. He likes to write about his trail experiences but finds it more rewarding to have trail experiences.

Marion Davison
Apple Valley, California

Marion is a member of the Pacific Crest Trail Association. She has completed more than 400 miles of the Pacific Crest Trail, which she and her husband are hiking in sections during weekend, week-long, and month-long trips. She is also a Boy Scout leader and usually hikes with a small band of Scouts.

Luca de Alfaro
Palo Alto, California

Luca is originally from Torino, Italy. While in Italy, he hiked in the Italian Alps, mostly in the Aosta Valley region. His Italian trips usually consisted of one-day or two-day hikes, the goal being to reach a mountaintop or pass. Among the many ascents that he has made, he is most fond of his climbs of Mount Emilius at age nine and of Mount Blanc at age fourteen. After moving to California, he and his wife, Françoise, discovered the joys of multiday hikes. He has backpacked numerous times in Yosemite and Sequoia national parks.

Corinne Edwards
Willington, Connecticut

Corinne thru-hiked the entire Pacific Crest Trail in 1996.

Lou Ann Fellows
Grand Canyon, Arizona

Lou Ann was one of the original end-to-end North Country Trail thru hikers, and helped to make the trail declared a national scenic trail in 1978. Following a serious injury on the trail, she was one of only two to finish the North Country Trail that year. Lou Ann presently works as a nurse at Grand Canyon National Park, where she often hikes.

Pete Fish
"Pickax Pete"
Ventura, California

Pete retired in 1990 after thirty-three years as a geologist with Chevron. He hiked the entire Pacific Crest Trail in four segments during the years 1991 through 1994. He is presently on the board of directors of the Pacific Crest Trail Association and also serves as the regional trail coordinator for southern California. He spends his retirement leading dozens of volunteer trail maintenance projects on the Pacific Crest Trail each year. Pete and his wife, Joyce, have three grown children and are proud grandparents.

Ron and Karen Forest
Manitou Springs, Colorado

Ron and Karen are members of the Pacific Crest Trail Association and have completed almost 900 miles of the Pacific Crest Trail.

Chet J. Fromm
Port Orange, Florida

Chet is a retired chief warrant officer of the United States Army. He has hiked the entire length of the Appalachian, Florida, North Country, and Pacific Crest trails, a total of more than 8,000 miles. He hopes to eventually thru-hike each of the remaining National Scenic Trails. His hobbies include backpacking, flying, painting, and working with computers. Chet is married and has four adult sons.

Steve Fuquay
"Switchback"
Las Vegas, Nevada

Steve has been hiking for nearly thirty years. He is retired from the federal government and currently teaches business at the local community college, using his summers for longer distance-hiking opportunities. He is a volunteer wilderness guide with the Bureau of Land Management and has written magazine and newspaper articles on the subject of backpacking.

Dan Gard
Missoula, Montana

Dan recently served as a backcountry ranger in Glacier National Park for two seasons and enjoyed many wilderness hikes while patrolling the trails. Prior to that, he worked in Yellowstone National Park for a number of years and logged more than a hundred miles each summer hiking throughout the park. He now is employed by the U.S.D.A. Forest Service as project coordinator for the Nez Perce (Nee-Me-Poo) National Historic Trail.

David and Sandra Geisinger
Schenectady, New York

David and Sandra are members of the Pacific Crest Trail Association and have completed more than 700 miles of the Pacific Crest Trail. Dave has been a local and national outings leader for the Sierra Club for more than twenty years. Dave and Sandra are also members of the Adirondack Mountain Club.

Craig Giffen
Portland, Oregon

Craig is a native of central Washington, but he left promptly after high school. While taking time off from college to pursue a degree in life, Craig fulfilled his desire to work in a music store and to thru-hike the Pacific Crest Trail. Craig completed the Pacific Crest Trail over the course of two summers, finishing the trail in 1996.

Benedict Go
"Ben Go"
Vallejo, California

Ben completed the entire Pacific Crest Trail in 1996. A wonderful trail cook, he was also known by his other trail name, "Ben Gourmet." Ben came to the United States from the Philippines in 1982. He is the author of the *Pacific Crest Trail Data Book.*

Brian Guldberg
Bozeman, Montana

Brian had completed 500 miles of the Pacific Crest Trail when a foot injury ended his planned thru-hike in 1994. Brian plans to return and complete the Pacific Crest Trail in the near future. For the past fifteen years, he has hiked in the Rockies, the canyon country of the southwestern United States, and the mountains of New Zealand, Alaska, and Canada.

Joe and Claire Hageman
"Mongoose and Buttercup"
Trenton, North Carolina

Claire and Joe have hiked sections of the Appalachian Trail and are planning a thru-hike for the near future. They backpacked the Grand Canyon in 1995 and Glacier National Park in 1996. They also enjoy wilderness canoeing and have paddled the waters of the Boundary Waters Canoe Area Wilderness and Adirondack Mountains. They are vegetarians and therefore have to use additional imagination when planning their menus. "We are constantly trying new recipes on our trips."

Jeffrey Hare
Citrus Heights, California

Jeffrey is part of a hiking group that has made annual treks into the backcountry for a number of years. Each of the group's annual trips last about six days and cover approximately 50 miles. As a group, they have covered more than 150 miles of the Pacific

Crest Trail and many more miles on other trails. Their goal is to eventually complete the entire Pacific Crest Trail from Canada to Mexico. Jeff promises that if you ever meet him in the wilderness, he'll be happy to share a slice of his trail pizza.

Debbie Higgins and Peter Sandiford
"The Canadians"
Quebec, Canada

Debbie and Peter thru-hiked the entire Pacific Crest Trail from Canada to Mexico in 1995.

Kevin Hobart
"Blue"
Mount Vernon, Washington

Kevin has completed more than 800 miles of the Pacific Crest Trail.

Jim Hoeferlin
Charlotte, North Carolina

Jim is married and the father of two children. He works in the finance department of Michelin Aircraft Tire Company. He has hiked approximately 700 miles of the Appalachian Trail as well as the Pacific Crest Trail from Walker Pass to Mount Whitney, a distance of about 100 miles.

Kirk Ikens
Rogers City, Michigan

Kirk has completed more than 900 miles of the Pacific Crest Trail.

Diane King
Somers, Connecticut

Diane is a farmer. In 1996, on her very first long-distance backpacking trip, she thru-hiked the Pacific Crest Trail solo from Canada to Mexico. Diane looks forward to hiking the Continental Divide Trail someday.

Jack Konner
Beaverton, Oregon

Jack is married and lives near his children and grandchildren in Oregon. He has completed more than 200 miles of the Pacific Crest Trail. Jack is a member of the Mount Hood Chapter of the Pacific Crest Trail Association. For several years now, he has led work crews on the Pacific Crest Trail in Mount Hood National Forest and the Columbia Gorge National Scenic Area.

Martha Manzano
Falls Church, Virginia

Martha recently began thru-hiking the Appalachian Trail and plans to do the same on the Pacific Crest Trail in the near future.

Ann Marshall
Port Orchard, Washington

Ann is a member of the board of directors of the Pacific Crest Trail Association. She has completed more than 1,000 miles of the Pacific Crest Trail. She is a member of The Mountaineers as well as editor/publisher of *Pack and Paddle* magazine.

Mark Morse
Anza, California

Mark thru-hiked the Pacific Crest Trail in 1998. While completing his Pacific Crest Trail trek, Mark wrote the following during a layover in Tehachapi, California: "This is my first attempt at such a journey, and I am loving every minute of it. Well maybe not the blisters, snowstorms, days spent in wet clothes, and 20-mile days with a 40-pound pack. But other than that, it's the best time I could imagine. God bless the people who keep such a trail possible for us; and thank you, Lord, for the body and mind to make this trip possible. Eat well and walk on!"

Will O'Daix
"The Green Ghost"
Indianapolis, Indiana

Will is a Pacific Crest Trail Association member and has hiked approximately 100 miles of the Pacific Crest Trail. He has spent time walking numerous other trails as well. Will is also a member of the Appalachian Trail Conference, American Long Distance Hiking Association, and Continental Divide Trail Association.

Geoff O'Hara
Honolulu, Hawaii

Geoff began section-hiking the Pacific Crest Trail in 1997.

Allmuth Perzel
"Curly"
Tolland, Connecticut

Allmuth thru-hiked the entire length of the Appalachian Trail in 1992 in 180 days and the entire Pacific Crest Trail in 1996 in 166 days. She was born in Germany in 1940 and came to the United States in 1960. She graduated from Springfield College with a master's degree in Physical Education. Allmuth is married and has two sons. She believes that "you are never too old to hike any trail."

Alyssa Pinkerton and Jean Capellari
Allen Park, Michigan

Alyssa and Jean have completed more than 150 miles of the Pacific Crest Trail.

Irwin Reeves
Beaumont, California

Irwin has completed the John Muir Trail twice and finished half of the trail on a third trip. He is a member of the Pacific Crest Trail Association. Most of his hiking experience has been in the San Jacinto and San Gorgonio Mountains of southern California and the eastern flanks of the Sierra. He works in a hospital as a chemical laboratory scientist.

Dan and Sara Rufner
San Diego, California

Daniel and Sara have recently married and just graduated from college. They thru-hiked the entire Pacific Crest Trail in 1996. In 1998, they thru-hiked the Continental Divide Trail.

Craig Smith
"Smitty"
Springfield, Missouri

Craig has been a backpacker for nearly thirty years. He has trekked the Rockies from New Mexico to southern Montana and spent three months in the Santa Catalina range north of Tucson, Arizona. The recent addition of a new son to the Smith family will keep Craig's trips a little closer to home, but he does hope to begin section-hiking the Pacific Crest Trail in the not-too-distant future. Craig is married and his entire family loves camping and backpacking. He is presently head of public services for the F. W. Olin Library at Drury College. "I find ways to replicate meals in the wild that approximate what I cook at home. Hardest thing I ever cooked up while backpacking was roasted Cornish hens. Took too long."

Joe Sobinovsky
Citrus Heights, California

Joe is the administrative assistant for the Pacific Crest Trail Association. He thru-hiked the Appalachian Trail in 1988 and the Pacific Crest Trail in 1995. You won't want to miss Joe's exciting recipe for ham sandwiches.

Peg Spry
Agua Dulce, California

Although not a long-distance hiker, Peg is a strong supporter of the Pacific Crest Trail section that runs through her hometown. She plays a vital role for the long-distance hiking community by serving as a trail host and taking in and taking care of many of the backpackers who come through on their way north or south along the Pacific Crest Trail. Peg is a member of the Pacific Crest Trail Association.

Lee Terkelsen
Visalia, California

Lee is the editor of the Pacific Crest Trail Association's newsletter, *The Communicator.* Lee has traveled the Sierra Nevada extensively. He produced the videos *Somewhere Along the Way*, detailing two brothers' thru-hike of the entire Pacific Crest Trail, and *The John Muir Trail*, a high-quality documentary covering the geography of the trail.

Kurt Thompson
San Ramon, California

After several years of camping in the Oregon coastal rain forest, Kurt took up backpacking while at the University of Oregon. Backpacking 101, to his good fortune, fulfilled part of his physical education requirements. Kurt is a technical writer for Oracle Corporation, a software company based in Redwood Shores, California. Kurt completed a solo trip around the circumference of South Sister in Oregon recently and plans to hike a section of the John Muir Trail soon.

Roy Tryon
California City, California

Roy was born and raised in the Selkirk Mountain wilderness country on the Canadian border in Washington. Roy is an old redneck hillbilly stuck in the Mojave Desert, where he passes too much of his time as an architect at NASA's Dryden Flight Research Center at Edwards Air Force Base. A Boy Scout leader for ten years, he still anticipates the next campout or backpack trip up into the nearby Southern Sierra with his two teenage sons. Too many beautiful trails and campsites and not enough time!

Bob and Joy Turner
"Bob 'n' Bug"
Coeur d'Alene, Idaho

Bob 'n' Bug are a father-daughter team who thru-hiked the entire Pacific Crest Trail in 1997. They have also completed the Wonderland Trail.

Julia Vogel
Pasadena, California

Julia is a costume designer for commercials, theater, and musicians. She recently attempted to solo-summit the top fifteen highest peaks in Ecuador. She completed a solo trip of the John Muir Trail in 1996.

Jeff and Chris Wall
Lancaster, California

Jeff and Chris are experienced long-distance equestrians and compete at the national level in endurance competition. They regularly take their horses for strolls on the nearby Pacific Crest Trail. Jeff is a financial agent with United Services Planning Association.

Mark and Jen Watson
"Doc and Thumper"
Mechanic Falls, Maine

Mark has enjoyed hiking for as long as he can remember. Now that he has his own family, he takes the whole gang backpacking. They recently completed hiking a stretch of the 100 Mile Wilderness in Maine.

Chris Woodall
Simpsonville, South Carolina

Chris is a graduate student at the University of Montana. He thru-hiked the Appalachian Trail in 1992 and has completed nearly two hundred miles of the Pacific Crest Trail in the vicinity of Mount Whitney and Yosemite National Park.

John Woodall
Simpsonville, South Carolina

John is a technical manager for Michelin Tire Corporation. He is married and the father of two children. He thru-hiked the entire Appalachian Trail in 1992 and has completed a section of the Pacific Crest Trail in the Sierra Nevada.

Ben York
Alpine, California

Ben is past president of the Pacific Crest Trail Association. He is a graduate of the University of California at Davis and a retired veterinarian, practicing in the Imperial Valley for more than thirty years. After retiring, he and his wife, Adeline, attempted to complete the entire Pacific Crest Trail on horseback in 1992. Adeline had to leave the trail after breaking her arm near Big Bear, and Ben went on to complete the trail by himself. In 1996, he completed nearly 1,900 miles of trail on horseback. He is past president of the Back Country Horsemen of California, a member of the board of the San Diego Council of Trails, and an active Rotarian for nearly forty years.

Valerie York
Alpine, California

Valerie served as executive secretary of the Pacific Crest Trail Association for several years. Valerie was well-known to thru-hikers as she served as a conduit for trail condition information for the entire length of the Pacific Crest Trail. As a trail volunteer, Val describes herself as "talented with the loppers and a decent brush flinger." She holds a master's degree in Human Resource Education from Boston University. She is an opera singer who has spent nearly ten years training in Europe. Says Val, "Yes, I am trained in opera, but everyone seems to want to hear my rendition of 'Cow Patty.' Sigh."

Alan Young
Scottsdale, Arizona

Alan recently completed his second term as president of the Pacific Crest Trail Association. To pay his bills, he is also president of Netzel West, a management, long-range planning, and fund-raising consultant firm. He graduated from the University of Wisconsin in 1978 and earned his master's in Business Administration from Pepperdine University in 1989. He was one of the original thru-hikers of the Pacific Crest Trail, completing the entire trail in 1979.

Joan Young
Scottville, Michigan

Joan and Chips, her hiking dog, are accumulating miles on the North Country Trail. She has completed more than 1,000 miles on her quest to walk the entire trail. Friends accompany them on adventures ranging from day hikes to multiweek backpacking trips. Joan serves on the board of the North Country Trail Association and is a regular contributor to its newsletter, *The North Star*. She is also a member of the Florida Trail Conference. To support her hiking habit, Joan works part-time as coordinator of the Created Wetland project.

About the Authors

Christine Conners is an accomplished backpacker and outdoor enthusiast and a graduate of Outward Bound. She holds a master's degree in Psychology and formerly worked in the field of child, marriage, and family therapy. She is currently authoring several children's books that teach outdoor skills. In addition to her roles as author and mother, she is a part-time teacher of psychology.

Tim Conners has hiked more than 1,000 trail miles, many of which were on the Pacific Crest Trail and the High Sierra's John Muir Trail. While living in the Tehachapi Mountains of California, he served as a volunteer trail maintenance coordinator for the Pacific Crest Trail Association. He holds a bachelor of science degree in Aerospace Engineering and is employed by a major aircraft engine manufacturer.

Christine and Tim live in Cincinnati, Ohio, with their three small children, James, Michael, and Maria. It is their hope to one day thru-hike the 2,635-mile-long Pacific Crest Trail, so they are anxiously awaiting the day when their children are old enough to carry not only their own backpacks but their parents' as well!

Index

Packable Trailside Cooking Instructions

The following section contains the on-the-trail cooking instructions for each recipe in this book requiring final preparation in the backcountry. This section is intended to be torn out and taken along on the trip. You can either tear out the entire section and create your own lightweight, packable book of trailside cooking instructions or cut out individual instructions and place the slips of paper in your bag of ingredients or another convenient place in your pack. The Packable Trailside Cooking Instructions are also available online at www.Falconbooks.com/lipsmackin. Reference the Packable Trailside Cooking Instructions by recipe name.

Packable Trailside Cooking Instructions

Pacific Crest Pancakes

For each serving, melt 1 tablespoon Crisco in pan. Add ½ cup water to one bag (½ cup) of mix. Knead mixture in bag. To cook, spoon or pour pancake batter into greased cooking pan. Turn once. Since pancakes can burn easily on backpacking stoves, adjust the flame to its lowest setting and be prepared to hold the pan above the flame if it gets too hot.

Whole-Wheat Palisades Pancakes with Syrup

To make one serving, melt 1 tablespoon butter in pan. Remove brown sugar bag from bag of pancake mix. Add approximately ½ cup water to pancake mix. Knead bag until lumps are gone. Cut a large hole at one corner of the bag and pour batter into pan. Watch pancakes carefully and flip when the first side has browned. To make the syrup, add 1 tablespoon water to brown sugar bag and knead mixture until all lumps disappear.

Blue Ridge Blueberry Pancakes

For each serving, pour ¼ cup water and ¼ teaspoon oil directly into one bag of pancake mix and knead mixture well. Let stand for 15 minutes. Grease skillet and place over medium heat. Cook pancakes until brown on the bottom and bubbling on top. Turn pancakes and cook until other side is light brown. Serve with syrup, if desired.

Cameron Canyon Caramel Rolls

For two servings, add ½ cup water to one bag biscuit mix. Knead dough in bag. On low heat, melt 2 tablespoons of butter in a frying pan, preferably one having a nonstick surface. Add sugar and pecans to butter and stir. Cut a hole in the bottom of the biscuit bag and squeeze out dough as thinly as possible on top of pecan/brown sugar mixture. Cover entire pan and allow to cook. Check frequently to ensure that caramel is not burning. Dough will eventually become biscuitlike. After allowing rolls to cool, eat directly out of the pan.

Backcountry Cinnamon Rolls

This recipe requires a backpacking oven. For two servings, add margarine to the sugar-cinnamon-nut mix and mush together. Add ⅓ cup water to Bisquick-buttermilk mix and knead in bag. Take the dough out of the bag, place on a flat surface, and work it into a square about 10 to 12 inches wide and ¼- to ⅛-inch thick (thinner is better). Spread the sugary paste evenly over the dough. Roll the dough into a log. Cut the log into 1-inch-wide portions and place slices side by side in your backpacking oven. Follow directions specific to your particular oven, and allow to cook until the rolls rise and become firm. Remove from the stove and let cool.

Big River Apricot Granola, Goose's Multigrain Granola, Backpacking Cereal, Kooger's Wolf Creek Granola, Lost Valley Granola, Gravel Road Granola

Eat as is, or with powdered milk and water, either hot or cold.

Cherry-Walnut Couscous Porridge

For two servings, bring 1¼ cups of water to a boil. Stir in dry porridge mix, then cover and remove from heat. Allow to sit for 10 minutes. Stir and serve.

Mountain Corn Cakes

For two servings, add ⅓ cup water to the mix, seal the bag, and knead well by pressing and squeezing the bag. Melt butter in pan or skillet over a very low flame. Place large, heaping spoonfuls of the batter in your pan or skillet. The batter will spread some, so leave a little room between each, or cook one at a time. When bubbles appear all over the surface, carefully flip the cake onto the uncooked side. Cook another 30 to 40 seconds, or until the cake sounds hollow when lightly tapped.

Cornmeal Mush

For one serving, bring ¾ cup of water to a boil, add 1 tablespoon butter, and slowly add one bag of cornmeal mush mix. Stir while heating for 1 minute. Take off heat and wrap entire pan in towel or other insulator for 3 to 5 minutes before eating.

Appalachian Apple Bannock

Add 2 tablespoons of water to one bag of Bisquick-dehydrated apple mix, then knead bag until dough is slightly thinner than normal biscuit dough. Melt 1 tablespoon of butter in frying pan. Drop biscuit-size blobs into pan. Flatten slightly with spatula. Cook on low heat, turning once.

"Scrambling Up the Sierra" Eggs

For two servings, add 1½ cups water to the egg mixture and mix until the lumps disappear. Let sit for 5 to 10 minutes. Place 1 tablespoon of butter in frying pan and heat over a low to medium flame. Pour eggs into pan, scramble, and cook.

Kitchen Creek Breakfast Rice

For one serving, bring 1¼ cups of water and ¼ teaspoon of salt to a boil. Add remainder of ingredients, then cover and simmer 10 minutes or until rice is tender.

Chicken Curry Salad

The night before you plan to eat this meal, place ¾ cup of water into one bag (one serving) of salad mix. Keep salad at the bottom of bag and roll up the bag like a burrito to help keep it from leaking. Allow to sit overnight. In the morning, check how the rehydration is progressing and, if necessary, add more water. The salad should be fully rehydrated by lunch. At lunchtime, stir in a sixth of your seasoned oil into a serving of salad.

Creamy Cilantro Tuna Salad

The evening before having this salad for lunch, add 1 cup of water to one bag (one serving) of salad. In the morning, check to see how the rehydration is progressing and, if necessary, add more water. At lunchtime, add a fourth of the dressing and the contents of one mayonnaise packet.

Sierra Szechwan Chicken Salad

The night before you are ready to eat this meal for lunch, add ¾ cup of water to one bag (one serving) of the noodle mixture. Allow to sit overnight. Periodically toss the water around in the bag. In the morning, check to see how the rehydration is progressing and, if necessary, add more water. By lunchtime the meal should be completely rehydrated. You can eat it at room temperature, allow it to chill a few minutes in a cold river, or heat it briefly over a stove.

Tropical Trail Salad

Before hitting the trail, add 1 cup water to one bag of rice mix. Seal bag well. Salad will be ready by lunchtime.

Smitty's Lunch at Lost Lake.

Fold each piece of cheese in half twice. On each cracker, place a piece of cheese, then a bit of sardine.

White Mountain Tortillas

Mix hummus with 1½ cups of water. For each tortilla, heat 1 tablespoon of oil in pan. Place a fourth of the hummus on top of one tortilla and place one slice of cheese on top of hummus. Place tortilla in heated pan. Cover and cook until cheese has melted. Do the same to make the remaining three tortillas.

Trekker's Tabouli on Pita

To one bag (one serving) of tabouli mixture, add ⅓ cup of water and 1 tablespoon of olive oil. Allow to sit for about 2 hours. To serve, place one piece of cheese in one sliced pita. Cut a large hole in the bottom of the tabouli bag and squirt the tabouli into the pita. No cooking is necessary.

Tuna-Spinach Couscous

Add 1 cup water to one bag (one serving) of couscous. Mush around a bit, then let sit for 1 hour before eating.

Peanut Butter and Raisin Roll-ups

Spread half the peanut butter on each tortilla. Add raisins to each. Roll up and eat!

Simmering Pot Fruit Soup

For two servings, bring fruit to a boil in pot with 3 cups of water and simmer for 10 minutes (longer if you can spare the fuel). Turn off heat. Mix 1 cup water with lemon pudding in a plastic bottle until dissolved. Mix with fruit soup and serve in cups.

Domeland Nachos

For one serving, cut one tortilla into pie slices. Cut cheese into thin flat pieces. Heat 2 tablespoons of oil in frying pan. Place tortilla slices in pan with hot oil. Allow one side to cook, then flip. Drop pieces of cheese onto tortillas and cover pan, if possible. Heat on low until cheese melts. Cook other tortilla the same way.

Wagon Mound Tortilla Chips

For one serving, heat 5 tablespoons of oil in frying pan. Cut tortillas into pie slices. Place in hot oil. Fry until light brown and crispy on one side, then turn over and repeat on opposite side. Add salt when both sides are finished cooking.

Hawk Mountain Roll-ups

For one serving, stir bean mix with ½ cup of water. Let sit a few minutes until mix is fully rehydrated. Grate or chop 1 ounce of cheese. Spread bean dip on a tortilla with cheese and roll it up.

Piute Mountain Pizza

For one serving, add ⅓ cup water (more if needed) to Boboli mix in resealable bag. Knead the bag to help rehydrate the sauce. Cut cheese into small pieces. Heat oil in frying pan. Cut a 3-inch slice into the side of each whole pita, enough to cause the inside to separate. Once the sauce sufficiently rehydrates, cut a small hole in the corner of the bag and shoot the sauce into the holes of each pita. Stuff your cheese into the pita along with anything else you'd like to add. Place in the hot frying pan over medium heat and cook both sides. You can cover pan, but make sure the pitas don't burn. When cheese is melted, it's ready.

Kirk's No-Cook Pizza

For one serving, add ⅓ cup water (more if needed) to the resealable bag containing the Boboli. Knead until sauce rehydrates. This will take a few minutes. Spread sauce over the tops of both pitas and eat. No cooking is required.

Brower's Baco Spuds

For two servings, place a small amount of water into the dried vegetables and meat bag to rehydrate about 1 hour before cooking. Place 3 cups of water into your pot with only the veggie-meat ingredients and bring to a boil. Add the ingredients in the second bag and stir. Add extra water as needed. Mix gravy according to the directions on the package, and pour over the potatoes.

Irwin's Forester Pass Mashed Potatoes

For two servings, place 3½ cups of water in a pot. Rehydrate vegetables and TVP in water for about 1 hour. Bring water to a boil and add gravy. Stir continuously. Check vegetables occasionally and add additional water as needed to rehydrate. Add powdered mashed potatoes to mixture and stir.

Thru-Hiker Veggie Spaghetti

Begin rehydrating the spaghetti leather 1 hour before dinner. Place one serving of leather and 1¼ cups water in a sealable plastic container. It will rehydrate faster if you rip the leather into pieces. Carefully place container back in your pack and walk your last hour.

When you are ready to eat, bring 1¾ cups of water to a boil. Break in half one serving of the pasta and add to water, stirring for 2 to 3 minutes or until al dente. Drain any remaining water. Next, you have two options: either dump the hot pasta into the rehydrated sauce in your plastic container and eat it lukewarm, or dump the sauce into the pot of pasta and heat all the way through.

Ballou's Turkey Spaghetti

For each serving, simply add enough water to barely cover the spaghetti in a pot and bring to a boil. Some presoaking may be desirable at very high elevations.

Speedy Spaghetti

For two servings, add 4 cups of water to the dehydrated sauce bag at least 1 hour before you are ready to cook. Mix from time to time. Add more water if needed. While waiting for the sauce to rehydrate, boil the noodles in 2 quarts water and drain. Set aside. With the sauce rehydrated, place it in a separate pot. Heat the mix and add additional water as required. Add noodles and serve.

Gard's Glacier Spaghetti

For one serving, cook spaghetti in 2 quarts water until done, then drain. Stir in 1 tablespoon of olive oil then add parmesan mixture. Mix thoroughly.

Smitty's Favorite Spaghetti

For two servings, chop garlic thoroughly, then bring 1 quart of water to a boil and drop in the spaghetti-pasta mix. The tomatoes and TVP will reconstitute in 5 to 10 minutes depending upon altitude. When the noodles are soft, add the seasoning mix and stir until all the powder is dissolved. Divide and eat.

White Trash Pasta

For one serving, pour all ingredients into 2½ cups of water and bring to a boil in a pot. Allow to simmer 5 to 10 minutes until the broccoli is rehydrated.

Outdoor Pesto Tortellini

For two servings, add ½ cup of water to vegetable-pesto sauce mix and knead in bag. Reseal bag so sauce doesn't dry, and allow it to sit for 30 minutes. Add more water if needed. After allowing vegetables to rehydrate, begin to boil a pot of water for the tortellini. Add the tortellini and boil until rehydrated and hot, then drain. Add vegetable-pesto sauce mix and oil to tortellini and stir over low heat (adding more water as needed).

Michigan Salmon Fettuccine

For two servings, place 3 cups of water in pan with salmon and allow to sit for 20 minutes. Bring to a boil and add the rest of the ingredients. Reduce heat and allow noodles to rehydrate for 5 minutes or more. Add more water if needed.

Tahoe Chicken Curry

For two servings, bring 2 cups of water to a boil along with both bouillon cubes. Add dried dinner mix. Allow to cook about 1 minute. Remove from heat and let sit 5 minutes, or until the rice is tender.

Cascade Valley Chicken and Rice

For two servings, add dehydrated chicken, peas, and bouillon to 2½ cups of water in a pot. Bring water to a boil. Add instant rice and stir well. Remove from heat. Cover and let stand 10 minutes. A pat of butter improves flavor.

Tamale Pie for Ungrateful Waifs

While setting up camp, place one serving of Bag A and 2 cups of water in pot and allow ingredients to rehydrate. Check periodically to see if you need to add more water to keep the ingredients rehydrating properly. When the contents of Bag A are rehydrated, add the contents of Bag B along with ⅓ cup of water. Heat slowly over a low flame, stirring continuously until thick. Shut off flame and cover. Let set for about 5 minutes. The pie will have the consistency of porridge.

Katahdin Tamale Pie

For two servings, pour tamale sauce mixture into pan along with 3 cups of water. Bring to a boil and allow to cook for about 3 minutes. Add ⅓ cup water to the bag of cornmeal mix, and mush around until it becomes a dough. Cut a small hole in one of the corners of your dough bag and squeeze the dough out evenly onto the top of the tamale sauce. Reduce the heat to very low, cover the pan, and steam for about 10 minutes. The recipe is ready when an inserted toothpick comes out clean. Be careful not to let the mixture burn.

Sandy's Weed Salad

Collect greens along the trail in a plastic sack and wash them in the streams. Cut them fine and place in a 1-quart plastic bag. Toss in 2 tablespoons of dressing. Pick the following fresh weeds and herbal greens gathered from the sides of the trail if they look clean and fresh: miner's lettuce, dandelion, plantain, yellow clock, sheep sorrel, lamb's quarter, red clover, chicory and chick weed, wild and prickly lettuce, and bull thistle.

Trail Oven Pizza To Go

For one serving, place ½ cup water in sauce bag, adding more if you have dehydrated vegetables. Knead contents of bag until reconstituted, about 10 minutes. Place ½ cup of warm water in pizza crust bag along with 1 tablespoon of oil. Knead for at least 1 minute. Allow dough to rise in bag for 5 minutes in a warm place. (In a cold environment, stick the bag in a warm place inside your jacket.)

At this point, follow the directions specific to the type of backpacking oven you are using, but basically the pizza dough goes on the bottom of the baking pan, and the sauce, as you might expect, goes on top of the dough. If your oven requires a bag, you may choose to fold your dough over your sauce and make a sort of calzone-type meal. Bake until bread dough is cooked through and the sauce is hot.

Night-after-Night No-Cook Bean Soup

For each serving, add 3 cups of water to the mix in a pot and allow to stand 1 hour if using hot water, 2 hours if cold water. May be eaten hot or cold.

Japanese Energy Soup

For one serving, bring 2½ cups of water to a boil. Add rice-tuna mix and stir frequently until rice is soft and tuna is rehydrated. Add water if needed.

Packer's Pea Soup

For each serving, bring 2 cups of water to a boil and add one serving of soup. Stir well.

Dog Food Soup

For two servings, add all ingredients to 1 quart of water and simmer until vegetables are rehydrated and noodles are cooked. Reduce the cooking time by taking the pot off the flame and letting it sit for 5 minutes before eating. Stir occasionally while cooking. If mixture gets too thick, add a little more water.

Vermilion Valley Vegetable Soup

In a pot, add one serving (one bag) of soup mix to 2½ cups of water. Bring to a boil and cook until vegetables are fully rehydrated.

Tree Frog Soup with Rattlesnake (for two servings)

Method 1: Chop up Spam into small pieces. Heat 4 cups of water in pan. Add soup mix and Spam to pan and eat when it's hot.

Method 2: Divide the soup back into the four cups you brought. Chop up Spam into small pieces and divide evenly into the four cups. Heat 4 cups of water and divide into each of the cups. Stir and eat when soup is rehydrated. (Saves pack volume and you don't have to clean the pot.)

Method 3: Divide the soup back into the four cups you brought. Chop up Spam into small pieces and divide evenly into the four cups. Pour about 8 ounces of water into each cup. Place cups in the sunlight and allow the solar rays to warm them. (Saves volume, messiness, and fuel!)

Lassen Volcanic Eruption Chili

For two servings, add 1 quart of water to 1 bag of chili contents and allow to rehydrate for about 1 hour. Add more water if needed. Once rehydrated, heat the mix in a pot along with the chili seasoning.

Smoky Mountain Chili

For two servings, combine all ingredients with 5 cups of water in a pot. Cook, stirring often, for about 15 minutes or until beans are soft. When cooking, you may have to stir almost constantly while holding the pot above the flame in order to keep the chili from scorching. It gets quite thick, so keep adding water as necessary.

Hotter-than-the-Mojave Chili

Add one serving of chili mix to 1½ cups of water and heat until chili mix is fully rehydrated.

Campo Corn Chowder

In a pot, add 2 cups of water to each serving of soup leather and let sit for 1 hour. Bring soup mix to a boil and cook until mix is fully rehydrated and smooth, stirring frequently. (You can also bring the soup mix straight to a boil without the 1 hour of rehydrating, but you will use a little more fuel in doing so.) Add more water if needed.

Alaskan Chipped Beef Sauce

For two servings, melt 2 tablespoons of butter in a pan and mix with the dry ingredients along with 1 cup of water. Heat and stir until thick.

You-Don't-Need-Drawings-To-Do-It Poached Trout

For 2 medium-size trout, add seasoning mix and 1 bouillon cube to a pan of water (ideally about the size of a large coffee can). Bring the water nearly to a boil so that the bouillon cube is dissolved and the liquid is an aromatic weak herb broth. Add trout and cover with water. (You may have to cut larger fish in half to fit most backpack cook pots.) When water returns to near-boiling, cover pan and allow fish to simmer on low heat for 2 minutes. Remove from heat and poach for 10 minutes until flesh is firm (white or light pink, depending on the species) and cooked through to the backbone. Trout is done when the filets on each side can be stripped off the bones easily. Strip off and discard the fins and their short bones.

Backpackers' Potluck

Place all ingredients, including 1 tablespoon of margarine, into 3 cups of water and allow to sit for about 30 minutes. Bring mixture to a boil and cook for 10 minutes. If the vegetables aren't sufficiently rehydrated, allow them to simmer a little longer.

Trail-Grown Sprouts

For four servings, soak seeds in water for approximately 24 hours. Pour into mosquito netting. Place in an opaque plastic bag in your pack for three days. At the end of three days, bring netting out into the light (hang from your pack) for an additional day or two and *keep moist*.

The Couscous Burrito of the Mighty San Gabriels

For each serving, boil ½ cup of water in a pot. Add one bag couscous-taco seasoning mix. When rehydrated, scoop onto two flour tortillas. Add one hot sauce packet per burrito along with some grated cheese.

Ozark Burritos

For one serving, add picanté-bean mix to 1 cup of boiling water. Allow to cook until beans are fully rehydrated. The end product will be similar to refried beans. Spread the bean mixture over two tortillas, sprinkle on the cheese, then roll up the tortillas up like a burrito and eat.

Falafel Burgers

For one serving, heat 1 tablespoon of oil in frying pan. Mix falafel, onions, and Parmesan with ⅓ cup of water. Form into two burgers and flatten into pan. Cook over medium heat until browned on each side.

Backpack Pot Pie

After you reach your camp, add ¼ cup water directly into Bag B and knead until it becomes a dough. Keep sealed. Next, pour the contents of Bag A into a pot along with water that covers the mix by 1 inch. Allow to sit for at least 30 minutes. While setting up your camp, check periodically to see if you need to add more water to keep the ingredients rehydrating. Once rehydrated, bring the contents of Bag A to a boil for about 2 minutes, making sure that the mixture doesn't dry out.

Reduce heat and pour the contents of Bag B on top of the contents of the pot. Either spoon the mixture on evenly and thinly or cut a hole at the bottom of the bag and squeeze the mix onto the chicken, being sure to smooth it out afterwards. Cover and let simmer until Bisquick is cooked. Eat directly out of the pot.

Cottonwood Lakes Corn Macaroni

For one serving, place ingredients in pot along with 2 cups cold water and stir. Place pot on stove and simmer until macaroni is soft.

The Honeymooners' Cheesy Ramen

For one serving, cook ramen noodles in 2 cups of boiling water until noodles are soft. Add ramen spice mix packet and stir. Cut 3 ounces of cheese into pieces, add to noodles, and cook until it melts.

Doctari's Tuna Casserole

For each serving, bring 1½ cups of water to a boil, then add one bag of casserole. Stir frequently.

Forest Bulgur Pilaf

For two servings, bring 2½ cups of water to a boil. Add bagged vegetable mix. Simmer for 15 minutes or until bulgur is soft and water is absorbed. Remove from heat, and top with Parmesan cheese or Mrs. Dash if you'd like.

Sundown Sausage Delight

For two servings, cut 2 ounces of sausage into small pieces. Bring 2¼ cups of water to a boil. Add rice mix and sausage to the water and return to a boil. Cover and cook over low heat until rice is tender.

Bear Ridge Scramble

For three servings, add 1½ cups water to the Nature Burger mix and knead in the bag. Heat 2 tablespoons of oil in pan. Add burger mix and scramble. Serve on tortillas.

Celebration Dinner

For two servings, bring 3 cups of water to a boil. Add ham mixture and allow to cook until noodles are soft and meat is somewhat tender. Add Parmesan cheese.

Ben's Chicken and Cheese

For two servings, add a little water to the chicken bag and allow to rehydrate in bag. Bring a pot of water to a boil and add noodles. Cook until tender. Drain water then add cheese sauce-buttermilk mix, 1 tablespoon of butter, and rehydrated chicken. Allow to simmer until hot.

Sweet Wenatchee Rice Dish

For one serving, bring 1½ cups of water to a boil. Add rice mix and 2 tablespoons of margarine. Stir, then let sit for about 5 minutes.

Bob 'n' Bug's Spanish Rice Fiesta

For two servings, add salsa to 1 quart water. Bring water to a boil while stirring to mix the salsa. Add rice-bean mix, stir, and remove from heat. Serve as a meal by itself or use flour tortillas to make burritos.

Brown Rice Bonanza

For one serving, bring 1½ cups of water to a boil. Chop garlic and place the ingredients in the water; stir well. Cover the pan and remove from the heat source. Let stand 10 minutes. The vegetables need the time to rehydrate, as the rice will fully cook in 5 minutes. Pass out the soy sauce.

Quick-and-Not-So-Dirty Bean Soup and Rice

For one serving, empty the contents of the bag into the original packing cup. In a small pan, bring 1 cup of water to a rolling boil. Add the boiling water to the dehydrated mix in the cup. Stir well and let stand for 6 minutes.

Carolina Spice Rice

For one serving, boil the rice in 1½ cups of water for about 10 minutes. Drain and pour cooked rice from bag into pot. Cut pepperoni stick into pieces and add to rice with soy sauce. Stir and it's ready.

Adirondack Stew

For two servings, bring 4 cups of water to a boil and add the stew mix. Boil 7 to 10 minutes until tender. Stir frequently.

Cascade Stew

For two servings, add stew mixture to 5 cups of water and bring to a boil. Stir frequently. Let boil about 10 minutes or so until vegetables are fully rehydrated. Add potato flakes and stir.

Oriental Takeout

For each serving, bring 3 cups of water and the contents of one bag of ingredient mix to a boil. If using beans, add an additional ½ cup of water. Cook until rice is soft. Add more water if needed.

Mountain Quesadilla

For one serving, add ½ cup water to the salsa mixture and allow to sit for about 1 hour, adding additional dribbles of water if needed. Once rehydrated, warm 1 tablespoon of oil in pan on very low heat. Place one tortilla in pan. Pour salsa mix on top. Chop tiny pieces of the cheese and place on top of this. Cover with the last tortilla. Brown each side until cheese melts.

Curried Vegetable Couscous

For one serving, bring 1½ cups water to a boil. Add vegetable-couscous mix to the boiling water and heat until reconstituted.

Beartown Couscous

For two servings, add vegetables to 2¼ cups of water and bring to a boil. When vegetables have rehydrated, add couscous mix and bring to a second boil. Remove from heat and let sit for a few minutes until couscous becomes soft. Add extra water if needed.

Italian Trail Couscous

For one serving, add all ingredients, as well as 1 tablespoon of oil, to 1½ cups of water. Let sit for 20 minutes. Bring to a boil then reduce heat slightly and stir frequently. The cooking time depends on the altitude, but normally takes about 3 minutes. When ready, the couscous should have the consistency of a moist paste.

Glazed Spam for Festive Occasions

For two servings, melt 1 tablespoon of butter in pan over medium heat. Add 1 tablespoon of water and ¼ cup of brown sugar slowly, stirring with your fork. Slice Spam into ¼-inch-thick cuts. Add Spam slices to pan, flipping once to allow both sides to brown. Don't let it burn!

Bulk-Building Bread-On-A-Branch

For each serving, add ¼ cup of water to one bag. Mix and knead the bag until the contents have the consistency of pie dough. Wrap dough along the peeled end of a (nonpoisonous!) branch in the form of a long, 6-inch blanket, and seal the end with a flap of dough. Hold over fire until golden brown. Slide or peel it off the stick to eat.

Chapatis (Indian Herb Bread)

For one serving, add ½ cup water to the contents of one bag and knead well. *Important:* Let sit for at least 1 hour, then knead well again. Heat pan until hot, add oil, and roll dough very thin to about the thickness of two credit cards; you can use your water bottle as a roller and the bottom of a pot as a rolling surface. Place thin dough in pan and cook, flipping often, until brown spots appear. Do not overcook.

Whole-Grain Trail Bread Mix

To make pan bread or biscuits: Melt 1 tablespoon of margarine in a pan. To one serving (one bag) of bread mix, add ⅓ cup water and 1 tablespoon margarine. Mix thoroughly. Either spoon out biscuit-size dough balls or pour entire bag of dough into a medium-hot frying pan. Cover pan until bread has risen some and is browned on one side. Flip and brown other side.

To make dumplings for soup: To one serving (one bag) of bread mix, add ⅓ cup water and 1 tablespoon margarine. Mix thoroughly. Drop by spoonfuls into bubbling soup. Cover and simmer for 2 minutes or until dumplings are thoroughly cooked.

To make pancakes or tortillas: Melt 1 to 2 tablespoons of margarine in a pan. Add ½ cup of water, 1 tablespoon of margarine to 1 serving of bread mix (1 cup), in a resealable plastic bag. Mix. Pour onto greased medium hot fry pan, brown on one side. Turn over and brown the other side.

Damper

For one serving, add ½ cup water to one bag. Knead ingredients into breadlike dough. No rising time is required. Remove mix and form into a ball. Bury the damper ball directly into the hot coals of a campfire and cover with coals. Wait about 20 to 30 minutes. The damper will rise like bread while cooking. Insert a thin stick into the ball to see if it is cooked through; if it extracts without traces of dough, the damper is finished. Remove the burnt exterior and eat the hot insides with butter or jam.

The damper ball can also be cooked in aluminum foil to reduce the burning of the crust. It can also be cooked in a pan with a lid, or wrapped around a (nonpoisonous!) branch and cooked like a sausage-on-a-stick.

Mountain Storm Chocolate Glop

For one serving, slowly mix 1 tablespoon of water with cocoa mix into a thick blend. Heat 1 tablespoon of oil in pan. Add mixture to pan and fry. When it reaches the consistency of taffy, eat it straight from the pan.

Clear Creek Cinnamon Chips

For 2 servings, heat 4 tablespoons of oil in frying pan. Cut tortillas into wedges. Place tortillas in hot oil and fry for a short period of time before flipping. Remove and let cool. Toss fried tortillas into the bag containing the cinnamon-sugar mix. Shake and eat straight out of the bag.

Smitty's Apricot Brandy Flambé

In the morning of the day you plan to eat the flambé, add fruit to 1 cup of water in your wide-mouth bottle and carry with you throughout the day. After the evening meal, pour off the water or drink it. To make one serving, add ¼ cup of brandy to the fruit, recap the bottle, and shake well for about 1 minute. Divide into two bowls and be sure to share the liquid equally, or your trail partner may complain. Sprinkle sugar over the fruit.

Cache Peak Crumbles

For two servings, heat ⅓ cup of oil in pan. Add ⅓ cup of water to Bisquick-sugar mix and knead in the bag. Pour mixture from bag into a heated pan and start scrambling like you would with scrambled eggs, trying to get all the mix covered with hot, greasy oil. Donut crumbles are ready when they are a little crispy. Be careful when eating directly from the pan because of the hot oil.

Lazy Boy Roy's Biscuit-on-a-Stick

For two servings, add water (start with about ⅓ cup) to the Bisquick bag, seal it, and knead it with your hands to make a stiff dough. Add dribbles of water to bring the dough to a moist, but *not* runny, texture. Bite or cut a little hole in the bottom corner of the bag, and squeeze the dough out onto the cooking stick, in a candy-cane fashion while you slowly twirl the stick. (You can take the dough out of the bag to roll or shape it with your hands, but if you don't have any extra flour or oil in camp, this can get messy.) Make sure the dough is not too thick on the stick. Bake by turning biscuit-on-a-stick over the campfire or coals slowly until golden brown. Use live branches from nonpoisonous trees.

Whitewater Cheesecake

For four servings, add the 5 tablespoons of butter (preferably warmed; you can place it under your shirt on a cold evening to soften it) to the bag containing the crust mix. Knead the bag. Divide the crust mixture and pat it into the bottom of four individual cups. If you don't have any butter, you can simply pour the crust mix onto the bottoms of the cups.

To the bag containing the cheesecake mix, add 1½ cups water. (The water must be cold, or the pudding mix may not congeal properly.) Knead bag to eliminate clumps in the mix, and then shake the bag for 3 minutes, ensuring that the seal stays tight. Cut a small hole at the bottom of the bag, and squeeze the cheesecake mix into the crust of the four separate cups. Allow mix to jell, then eat out of cups.